Dear Bunny

I hope you enjoy
this as much as I do

Love
Pat & Clara

For All Who Love the Game

Lessons and Teachings for Women

Harvey Penick

with Bud Shrake

A Fireside Book
Published by Simon & Schuster

FIRESIDE
Rockefeller Center
1230 Avenue of the Americas
New York, NY 10020

First Fireside Edition 1999

FIRESIDE and colophon are registered trademarks
of Simon & Schuster, Inc.

Designed by Irving Perkins Associates

Manufactured in the United States of America

10   9   8   7   6   5   4   3   2

Library of Congress Cataloging-in-Publication Data is available.

ISBN 0-684-80058-6
ISBN 0-684-86734-6 (Pbk)

Contents

Introductions   11

Foreword   15

Lessons in the Afternoon   21

Helping It Up   26

Hit It Hard   29

Judy's Grip   34

A Practice Procedure   36

Three Games in One   37

The Card Table—Under and Under   39

The Card Table—Under but Over   40

A Fundamental   41

Picking a Putter   42

A Call in the Night   43

A Story by Helen   44

The Picture Show   47

Swing Thoughts   47

How to Have Both Golf and a Marriage   49

What's Your Hurry?   50

Playing the Breaks   51

The Best   53

A Champ and Her Children   54

A Golf Tip   58
The Vital Long Chip Shot   59
How Many Wedges?   61
Get a Feeling Fit   62
A Matter of Touch   63
No More Whiffs   65
The Lady in the Bunker   67
A View from the Window   71
Steady Head   72
Practice at Home   74
Practice the Short Ones   76
The Wright Way   77
Starting Your Swing   78
Let's Call Harvey   79
Be Yourself   81
Good Posture   84
Charging Betsy   84
My Banquet Speech   86
An Outlook on Putting   87
Thin Air   89
Keep at It   90
An Aspirin for Sarasota   93
Women's Tees   97
Refresh Yourself   98
The Basic Shot   99
Learning   100
How Much Is Enough?   101

Labor Day 102

She Does It All 104

A Cure for Mary Ann or Anyone Else 106

The Cactus Patch 107

The Left Wrist 108

Loft Is Your Friend 109

Strike It 110

Quick Cure 111

Swing Weights 112

Earl's Pearl 112

Skip the Details 113

Ruthe the Champ 114

Big-Chested Women 116

Women's Grips 117

Rolling with Mary Lena 118

Positive Attitude 119

Use What Fits 120

A Romance 121

Post It 122

Universal Advice 123

A Story by Mickey Wright 123

When to Offer Golf Advice to Your Spouse 130

A Story by Betsy Rawls 131

Enough Is Enough 133

Learn Etiquette from Barbara 133

Perceptions 135

Another Reason to Clip the Tee 135

Follow the Line   136
A Helping Hand from a Legend   138
Exercise   139
Listen to the Swish   141
Divots   142
Dropped at the Top   142
You Want Straight or You Want Far?   144
Alignment   144
Watch Your Step   146
Confidence   147
Advice from JoAnne   147
But We're Not Robots   148
Like a Violin   149
Home   151
About Betty Jameson   152
A Story by Paula Granoff   160
Uphill and Downhill   163
Scrambling   163
The Golf Ball Test   164
Where There's a Will . . .   165
Compliment from the Haig   166
Checking Ball Position   166
Big Enough   167
A Prayer   168
The Natural Way   169
Dressing   170
Remembering Babe   171

Know Your Own Game   172

Howdy Do   173

Playing Pregnant   174

Shut Your Eyes   175

A Mind Game   176

Patty's First Time   177

The Fifty-Yard Pitch Shot   178

Where Do Those Strange Shots Come From?   181

A Story by Susan Watkins   182

Nicole Remembers   185

Our Daughter Sandra   187

Introduction

by Betsy Rawls

When I heard that Harvey was writing another book, this time directed to women, I was delighted. Harvey has always been a wonderful teacher for everyone—men, women, kids, low-handicap amateurs, and professionals—but over the years he has had a special rapport with women. To men he was a mentor, a teacher, a friend; to women he was "God."

Whenever I talked to men about Harvey, they spoke of him with great respect and fondness. Whenever I talked to other women they all spoke about Harvey with reverence.

I don't know exactly what the difference was; I just saw that there was a very special relationship between Harvey and his women students. I could see also a little difference in Harvey when he taught women. He is a man of old-fashioned values and manners. He puts women on a pedestal and treats them with great care and with great caring. He is a little more gentle, a little more patient.

Through years of teaching, Harvey learned that a lot of women didn't have as many natural moves as men did. He understood that girls generally had not had the athletic training that boys had experienced because they hadn't played the boys' games. Harvey would comment that he couldn't say things like "swing the club like a weed cutter," because women had not swung weed cutters. He knew where to start with women—what they did naturally and what movements they had to be taught. He also knew what differences in a golf swing were due simply to strength. He would tell a football player things that he would not tell a housewife.

Harvey was always aware of individual strengths, weaknesses, and capabilities, aware of how different people should be taught, what limits people had. He knew what to change, what not to change, what was hard for women to do. His greatest strength as a teacher lay in his ability to see each pupil as an individual and to discern how that person should be taught to play golf.

The basic principles of a good golf swing apply to everyone. Everything Harvey says in any of his books is true for both men and women. But Harvey's genius lies in knowing what to tell women so that they can feel the correct swing, in knowing how to bring about the movements he wants, in knowing how to give women encouragement in developing a good golf swing.

Harvey made every woman feel as if her golf game was really important, and to Harvey it was. He took great pleasure in taking an unathletic woman and helping her play the game well enough to play comfortably with her friends and to truly enjoy the game. He has made the game of golf easier for his many women pupils and has made a very complex activity fairly simple. Harvey has brought thousands of women into the fascinating world of golf!

His special talent and insight come through in this book.

Introduction

by Kathy Whitworth

WHEN I WAS asked to write an introduction for this book, I was both flattered and very happy.

Harvey Penick has been and still is a big influence in my life. To be able to write a few words about him and his book is a real joy for me. When he wrote his first one—*Harvey Penick's Little Red Book*—I don't know who was more thrilled, Harvey or his students.

For years Harvey was reluctant to write anything for publication, because he worried that people who read his words might misunderstand, and he would hurt their game instead of helping it. So it was quite a surprise when he decided to share his wisdom with the rest of the world. But it was no surprise to me when his work turned out to be the best-selling sports book of all time.

Those of us who have had the privilege to know him and the good fortune to be given golf lessons by him are delighted that now, through his books, the golfing world can get to know and enjoy Harvey as we have.

Even if you have not read his first two books, you are in for a treat with this one. Just as the first ones were, this book is instructional, humorous, and philosophical. I guarantee it will help your golf game—and probably your outlook on life as well.

I could go on about how much Harvey means to me and why he has had such an impact on my life. But I feel that with these books, Harvey speaks for himself and will give to you just as he has given to me.

Enjoy.

Introduction

---

by Sandra Palmer

How BLESSED I have been to have Harvey Penick in my life!

His guidance, his patience, his sense of humor, his philosophy, and above all his love for people and for golf have been a great source of strength and inspiration for me.

I still feel the same excitement when I come see him today that I felt when I first came to him more than thirty years ago. Being a friend and pupil of Harvey's is truly special. I wish everyone, golfer or not, could have the experience of being in his company.

Harvey and his lovely wife, Helen, make this a better world by their presence.

Foreword

BOBBY JONES WROTE half a million words on golf and said he had nowhere near exhausted the subject. In my first book, I wrote a fraction as many words on the golf swing and the golfing life, and I thought that everything I know about the game was in those pages.

I was speaking of the fundamentals. But most of what is written about golf is commentary.

Golfers are always hungry for more commentary, and writers and teachers can always think of one more thing they should have said.

Bobby Jones knew golf in a way that I never will. As an international champion, he experienced the nerve and thrill of playing the game at a level that I, a grown caddie, a lifelong club pro and teacher, can only imagine. His descriptions of famous rounds at historical tournaments, his reflections on the strength of mind demanded of a champion, will last in literature as long as the game does.

His commentary is that of a genius player.

All golfers from high handicappers to experts are creators of their own commentaries on the game. Dreams, experiences, tales of glory and woe, desire, love and death, reflection, rapture—all these are among the commentary golfers bring into the pro shop and onto the practice tee.

My commentary is from the point of view of a teacher who has been at it so long I have worn out two Austin

Country Club golf courses and am now parking my cart under the live oak trees at a third.

Not long ago I was talking about golf with one of my favorite and most celebrated friends and pupils, Kathy Whitworth. We were sitting in the living room. My brave, long-suffering companion and wife, Helen, bless her, was talking on the phone in the kitchen.

People call from all over the world to talk about golf. Because I don't hear well enough to use the phone, gracious Helen must act as interpreter. Some calls are from famous people. Not taking anything away from the others, I believe Helen is most impressed so far by two phone calls from Paul Harvey. We have listened to him on the radio for what seems like fifty years.

Kathy is a teacher now. She wanted to know how I approach teaching golf to women. At the time she asked, Kathy was helping to teach a class of Japanese girls who had been sent across the ocean to Columbia Lakes, near Houston, to learn to become professional golfers. One of the girls had been playing golf for about a year. She was a champion swimmer and a wonderful athlete and hit the ball a long way, but she was having trouble understanding the short game.

"You've had great success teaching women. What can I do or say to get through to her?" Kathy asked.

We talked for half an hour about that Japanese girl.

Pupils don't realize it, but their teachers are thinking of them away from the golf course. I sit up many nights wondering how to help a pupil.

After Kathy left, I began to think about the women pupils I have been blessed to teach and the new women pupils who arrive regularly, and I thank God for making me such a lucky fellow.

Only thirteen women have been inducted into the

LPGA Hall of Fame, one of the most select groups in sports. Five of them have practiced their swings with me. A sixth was my pupil briefly, before her father decided to take her to a different venue.

I have always loved teaching women. From Hall of Fame champions to the wife who wants to learn to play golf with her husband when they go on vacation, or the businesswoman who wants to play the game with her clients, or the women comrades who make the regular foursomes, or the college girl trying to win a place on her team—they all intrigue me.

I am just as excited by a well-struck shot from the wife or the businesswoman or the club regular or the college girl as by a perfect shot from the Hall of Fame player.

Most women sense that I want so much to help that I become the one who is nervous, and the woman pupil is free to put her mind to performing the motions we want without fear of being judged harshly by me. I tell them, "Be at ease. You won't do anything I haven't seen before."

As everyone knows, all good golf swings are alike in that the club must make certain motions as it passes through a short space. The angle and speed of the clubface at the moment it strikes the ball are the test all swings must take.

The golf club doesn't care if it is being swung by a woman or a man.

But teaching a woman to do this is a different experience from teaching a man.

My friend Tommy Armour, famous player and teacher, wrote, "In my many years of experience, the difference in teaching men and women has always been a great problem. Although both male and female have two legs and two arms, their structures differ, and inescapably men are much stronger and generally have greater athletic ability than women. I have always found it very difficult to adjust myself mentally to these differences. And, as I think most pros will tell you, they make golf instruction a very difficult task."

Women have characteristics that must be taken into account. A typical problem for women players is distance. I almost always try to give women more distance, more power.

I don't change my fundamental teaching because I have a woman pupil—but I do change my commentary.

I am happy to learn that half the people taking up golf today are women.

I shudder to imagine the bad advice these women are getting from husbands and fathers and boyfriends, most of whom should keep their minds on the vexations of their own game.

A woman who wants to learn golf should go see a qualified professional teacher as soon as possible.

If no pro is available to you and you want to know what I teach to women pupils, then please let me try to help you with my lessons and commentary in this book.

Explaining the inexhaustible need for commentary, Bobby Jones wrote: "One reason golf is such an exasperating game is that a thing learned is so easily forgotten, and we find ourselves struggling year after year with faults we had discovered and corrected time and again. But no correction seems to have a permanent effect, and as soon as our minds become busy with another part of the swing, the old defection pops up again to annoy us."

I think this is because words don't describe actions very well, and the more detailed the words, the more confused the muscles get when they try to follow the directions.

This is why I believe in simple teaching, putting simple pictures into the pupil's mind that make a vivid, long-lasting impression. The technical things take care of themselves when you remember and trust the pictures and feelings.

I hope teachers as well as pupils will call it time well spent to pay attention to the lessons and commentary in this book, for they come from my long life in the game.

The day I stop learning is the day I will quit teaching.

Harvey Penick
Golf Professional Emeritus
Austin Country Club, 1995

Lessons in the Afternoon

IT WAS EARLY on a hot Saturday afternoon in July. I had already been at the club watching Sandra Palmer hit balls for an hour or so. Now I was back at home in my lounge chair in the living room, feeling sort of achy and drained by the sun.

I thought I would have a bowl of soup and a sandwich for lunch. Then I would read my mail and answer a few letters before the Women's Open appeared on TV in a little while. Sandra was spending the weekend at our house, and she planned to come from the practice range to watch the tournament with me. Watching the Open while sitting with an Open champion like Sandra is a thrill for me. I knew it would pick up my spirits.

But my son, Tinsley, walked in the front door and said, "Dad, we need you at the club."

"What's the matter?" I asked.

"A woman needs your help."

"Does it have to be right now?" I asked.

"Dad, she has come a long way and is eager to see you."

Ordinarily what Tinsley had said would have roused me to get into my golf cart and return to the club at once. I could never turn down a woman in distress. On this day, though, with the temperature above one hundred degrees and several things at home I wanted to be doing, it was hard for me to think about moving.

"What seems to be her problem?" I asked.

"She can't get the ball into the air," Tinsley said.

That was all I needed to hear.

"Help me out of this chair," I said.

Teaching frustrated women golfers to hit the ball into the air is a challenge I love, one that when accomplished brings forth such a roar of joy from both the pupil and the teacher that I get goose bumps that make me feel I'm in the middle of an electrical storm.

An attractive woman was waiting in the practice area when I arrived in my golf cart. She introduced herself as Susan Baker. She said her husband, Jim, was out on the course playing golf. They lived back and forth between Houston and Washington, D.C., she said, but were in Austin to attend a wedding.

"Use your 7-iron and let me see you hit a few balls," I said.

What I needed to know first was whether her frustration was caused by the path of her swing or by the angle of her clubface.

Her swing looked pretty good to me, but every ball she hit rolled about thirty yards along the ground.

"I've had a number of lessons, and yet I just keep on doing this," she said.

I looked at her hands on the club. Her grip seemed reasonable. But having seen that her swing was all right, I knew her grip had to be the villain.

I asked her to remove her glove and take her grip again.

Sure enough, that is where the culprit lay concealed.

When she took her grip, both hands were pretty much under the handle. But then she twisted her flesh around so that her bad grip was disguised to look like a reasonable grip.

"Would you mind if we back up a little and start over?" I asked.

"Please do," she said.

"Let's forget the word 'grip.' Let's just think about placing your hands on the club. Please let me guide you into placing them. Look at how your hands hang naturally at your sides. Now place your left hand on the handle with a natural feeling so that you can glance down and see three knuckles. That's right. That's how I want it. Leave it just like that, without twisting. Now place your right hand on the handle so that your lifeline in your palm fits against your thumb. That's very good."

I leaned over and touched her left elbow.

"Let go of the tension in your elbows," I said.

Instead, she let go of the club with her hands. That always happens at first. I asked her to place her hands back on the handle as she had done before, without rolling her left arm or twisting her flesh. Just place her hands on the handle and hold it lightly.

I touched her left elbow again.

"Without letting go of the club, allow the tension to go out of your elbows and your shoulders," I said.

I saw her elbows soften. Her shoulders became less rigid.

I clapped my hands with approval.

"Now look at a spot on the grass and make me a nice practice swing, hitting the spot."

Susan made several good-looking practice swings that brushed the grass.

"Now put a tee in the ground," I said. "We don't need a ball yet. Just a tee. Please make me a nice swing and hit that tee. Feel that you are swinging easy, but hit that tee hard enough to cut if off or knock it out of the ground."

After Susan did this half a dozen times, clipping that tee with a good, smooth, full swing, I asked her to put a ball on the tee.

"Now, disregard the ball but go ahead and give that tee a healthy crack," I said.

Susan hit that ball out of my sight. My eyes are not as sharp as they once were, but I could tell she had hit it well over a hundred yards in the air with her 7-iron.

Susan screamed with pleasure. She jumped up and down. She leaped over and kissed me. I was tingling from head to toe.

"I never thought it was possible!" she said. "Let's do it again."

She did it several more times, cutting off the tee with a nice swing, the ball flying out there more than a hundred yards, plenty high with a little tail on it.

"Now, pull out your 3-wood," I said.

I saw a moment of fear in her eyes.

"Trust me," I said. "You know how to do it. Treat this club just as you have been treating the other one."

Well, what do you think happened?

With her 3-wood, Susan hit the ball 170 yards.

She was astonished. She was so thrilled that tears rushed to her eyes.

My arms turned white with goose bumps.

"Now, please listen to me," I said. "I want you to remember. What we did here today—or rather what you did—it works the same in Houston in or Washington, D.C., as it does at Austin Country Club. Always remember that, and you will be fine from now on."

I asked Susan to enjoy the game of golf to its fullest and please come back and see me anytime she thought she needed me.

"Please give my regards your husband," I said.

Driving me home in my golf cart, Tinsley said, "Do you know who her husband is?"

"Jim," I said.

"Her husband is James Baker. He was secretary of state and chief of staff for President Bush."

I am not a political person, but I do have a soft spot for President Bush. He wrote me a letter about golf and life that he hand typed himself. His letter is framed on the wall of my little bedroom at the front of the house. In the middle of the night when pain keeps me awake, I often look at that letter and pinch myself to be sure it's real, that a president sat down and typed a letter to a grown caddie.

Back at the house, Sandra was watching the Open on television. As I settled into my lounge chair again, Sandra caught me up on what had been happening.

The Swedish star Helen Alfredsson had started the Saturday round with a big lead on the field. But her game was faltering.

As I began watching, she was in the struggle of losing eight strokes to par in ten holes. It was painful to see. I felt sorry for her. Such things happen to even the best players, and all golfers know it. But still my heart went out to this handsome young woman who has so much talent.

All of a sudden, with several holes yet to play, the television network cut short my suffering on Helen Alfredsson's behalf, as well as what joy I would be receiving from the rise of Patty Sheehan and other fine players in the Women's Open—and my pleasure at listening to the TV commentary by Judy Rankin, who used to be a pupil of mine.

A man's voice on the television told us they were leaving the Women's Open because their time was up. The network switched to some kind of track meet in Russia.

"Do you think they would do that if this was the Men's Open?" Sandra said. "What if some prominent man player was losing a big lead, and some other prominent men players were making a charge? Would the network switch away to a track meet that was taped earlier in another country? Would they dare do that to men?"

"I don't think so," I said.

"You know darn well they wouldn't," Sandra said.

She headed toward the door.

"I'm going back to the practice tee," she said. "They won't let me watch the Women's Open, but they can't stop me from practicing."

So I read my mail and answered letters. It was too hot for anything else. But I felt better now than when I came home earlier in the day.

Remembering Susan Baker's cry of pleasure when she saw that ball fly out there 170 yards, I kept smiling. Moments like that make my life fulfilled.

And if enough Susan Bakers find joy and satisfaction in the great game of golf, maybe someday that network will treat the world's finest women players with the same respect it reserves for men.

Helping It Up

FOR SEVENTY YEARS as a teacher, I have done to nearly every women pupil one of the same things I did to Susan Baker.

I have touched them gently on an elbow and said, "Let go of the tension here."

The pupil's first reaction is to let go of the club.

This shows me that the woman thinks of her elbows as part of her grip.

When, as a novice, she starts trying to hit the ball, she tries to hit it with her elbows.

Why is this?

I think it is because girls were not brought up to swing at things with a stick.

In recent years, girls' participation in sports has grown enormously. A great many more girls now play baseball and softball in organized leagues. They learn to swing at a ball with a stick. The result is that I see young girls coming into golf who are good athletes and have been taught to use their athletic abilities rather than conceal them, as often happened in earlier days.

But even with many of these good young female athletes, I still need to tap them gently on an elbow and say, "Let go of the tension here."

I touch the elbow first. But if necessary—and it usually is—I will touch them on the shoulders also and say, "Let go of the tension here, too."

I believe women should underline these words in red ink: *Let go of the tension in your elbows and shoulders.*

It appears to me that women are naturally inclined to push rather than to swing or throw.

Instead of letting go of the tension in their elbows and forearms and shoulders, novice women golfers tighten up and put a stiff-armed pushing motion on the ball.

This pushing motion is tied in to the novice woman's desire to help the golf ball into the air.

As every golfer must learn before he or she can see improvement, the ball goes into the air when you give it a hearty spank. If you try to help lift it up, the ball will just roll along the ground.

I usually refrain from saying, "Hit down on the ball."

The reason I avoid that familiar golfing axiom is that I feel it may plant the wrong impression in the pupil's mind. By thinking "hit down," the pupil may start hitting down from the top of the backswing. Hitting from the top is one of the gravest sins in golf and one of the most difficult to put out of your life.

But the fact remains that you must hit down on the ball to make it go up.

On a good iron shot, you strike the back bottom of the ball at the bottom of the downswing to make the ball go up. It goes up because of the loft on your clubface.

On a good iron shot, you strike the back bottom of the ball just before the bottom of your swing. The ball will roll up the face of your club and fly into the air, while your clubface continues into the earth ahead of where the ball was and then rises into your follow-through. On a good iron shot, the clubface tears out a narrow strip of grass and dirt.

It is this cut-out strip of grass and dirt, the divot, that is the bane of many novice women golfers.

Women don't want to take a divot. They don't like to tear up the grass.

Mickey Wright said a psychiatrist cornered her after a tournament and demanded to know why women are afraid to take a divot.

"Are they?" asked Mickey. (As one of the top players in history, if Mickey was ever afraid of taking a divot, it would only have been when she was practicing on the living room carpet.)

"Yes, they are," the psychiatrist persisted. "And I know why. Women are afraid to take a divot because they don't want to damage the earth!"

I assure my pupils that the divot is a useful and harmless thing. The earth likes a good divot. I mean a good divot the size and shape of a dollar bill. The earth is less fond of those pie-plate divots some players take, but the earth accepts all divots as part of the game. The torn earth will soon replenish.

An expert can hit a good full shot without taking a divot, but this level of skill is far beyond most players.

You want to help the ball go up?

Let the tension go out of your elbows, arms, and shoulders and make a strong swing. The only way you can help the ball up is to hit it.

Hit It Hard

A WOMAN ARRIVED at the old Austin Country Club on Riverside one morning in an expensive foreign car that had California plates on it. With a vigorous stride she entered the pro shop and said, "Where would I find this man called Mr. Penick?"

I looked up from the notebook in which I was jotting reminders to myself about a pupil I had just been with.

I said, "Mr. Penick is my father. I am his son, Harvey."

"Which one of you is the teacher?"

"That would be me," I said.

"Well, come on then, Harvey. Let's get to work."

From her brassy voice and the way she walked, it was plain this woman was accustomed to being the boss. Not that I mind a woman boss, but it is wrong to start a golfing relationship with the student bossing the teacher.

"I'm working already," I said, gesturing toward my notebook.

"I mean I want you to do golf pro work and give me a lesson."

"I can give you a lesson without moving," I said. "The first thing you should learn is that golf is not work. Golf is a game. And I don't like how you use the word 'lesson,' as if it is something you are forced to do. If your mother makes you stay inside and study the piano when you had rather go swimming with your friends, that's a 'lesson.' "

A curious little smile crossed her lips, sort of surprised, as if maybe the caddie had just told her to carry her own bag.

She said, "Harvey, what is it you do if you don't give lessons?"

"I guide your learning," I said.

"Well, let's go start guiding and learning. I don't have all day."

"Why do you play golf?" I asked.

She was halfway out the door before she heard me. She stopped and looked back, wondering what kind of odd person she had stumbled upon in the Texas wilderness.

"Why?" she said.

"Do you play for exercise? For companionship? For business reasons? Do you play to keep your husband company? Do you play because you love the game?"

"I play for the competition. I want to beat the other women at my club, and the men, too, if I can."

I said, "How much time are you willing to spend practicing?"

"I play on Tuesdays with my friends and on Saturdays

with my husband and another couple. We have two kids in high school and one who goes to UCLA but lives at home. I own a chain of clothing shops and a string of horses, and that takes some time. But I guess I could practice two days a week, an hour at a time."

We went to the practice tee. I asked her to take a few practice swings with her 7-iron. As she stepped into a comfortable address position, I saw that she had a good grip.

Her practice swings were lovely—slow and rhythmical. I love an unhurried backswing. Bobby Jones's teacher Stewart Maiden told him, "You don't hit the ball with your backswing." I follow the philosophies of Maiden. Two teachers who had great influence on me are Maiden and his other famous pupil, Glenna Collet Vare.

The woman was still swinging slowly and gracefully, still warming up, I thought.

I stuck the peg in the ground. "I want you to use that sweet swing and clip off this tee," I said.

She used her sweet swing and hit the tee and never even bent it sideways before she finished in a well-balanced follow-through.

"Again," I said. "Hit it hard this time."

Same rhythmical swing slow all the way through. Her clubface hit the ground and didn't bounce, much less cut a divot.

"Is that hard enough for you?" she said.

This woman was trapped in her mirror.

She knew the fundamentals: feet, posture, ball position, grip, pivot. She knew the one-piece takeaway and the elbow back to the side in the downswing. A nice high follow-through with elbows up.

She looked wonderful, but she was a powder puff.

"How far do you hit a 7-iron?" I asked.

"About sixty yards."

Imagine. That lovely swing and such poor efficiency. She had learned the swing, but she hadn't learned to hit the ball. She cared more about looking good than about swatting her golf ball down the fairway.

"Do you have a worst enemy?" I asked, teeing up a ball for her.

"One?"

"One you'd like to really bash."

"Yes, I can think of one."

"This ball is that worst enemy you are thinking about. Go ahead and get mad and hit it as hard as you can."

"But the golf swing is supposed to be easy, not hard," she said.

" 'Swing easy but hit it hard' is what you are thinking of," I said, referring to the famous saying of Julius Boros. "But forget that on this swing. I want you to swing as hard as you can and bash your enemy with all your power."

The woman tried mightily to take a clout at that enemy, at the risk of losing some of her lovely swing motion, but she hit the ball about sixty yards.

"I got him that time," she said.

She thought she had hit the ball hard. She had no idea what hitting the ball hard meant. Worse, she had no golf muscles. She had no power in her nearly perfect swing, and it was because she had no golf muscles. She had a well-toned body, but not to play golf with.

"Hit a few balls," I said. "I'll be back soon."

In the golf shop I found an old 4-wood. I wrapped lead tape around the head to make it about as heavy as adding four silver dollars to it.

I went back to the woman at the practice tee. Sixty

yards away from her, the grass was peppered with balls she had struck gracefully with her 7-iron.

"All right, Harvey, what do you have to say?" she said.

"There's only one thing I can do for you," I said.

I handed the weighted 4-wood to the woman.

"Take this with you," I said. "Promise me you will swing this club ten times every day for three weeks. On Tuesdays and Saturdays, swing the club after you play golf, not before. After three weeks, I want you to increase your swings to twenty-five each day. Remember to keep a steady head while you swing and always aim at a certain spot. You will start to notice results in a few weeks. After you swing this weighted club twenty-five times each day for one year, you will be in the championship flight at your club."

She hefted the club uncertainly. "Really? Why?"

"Swinging this club will build your golf muscles. As your muscles get strong and trained in what to do, you will automatically start swinging the club faster. You will be swinging easy and hitting it hard. If you will keep up this exercise for the rest of your life and spend most of your practice time around the green, you will become your club champion. You will beat everybody."

She made a couple of easy passes with the weighted club. It was making sense to her. I knew she would have the discipline to continue swinging the weighted club, and it would combine with her lovely swing to make her a long hitter.

"I'm going back to the shop now," I said.

"This is the end of the lesson?"

"It's a guide to learning," I said. "You're going to become your own teacher."

"When should I come see you again?"

"You'd be welcome anytime, but I doubt if you will

33

ever need to see me again," I said, leaving her on the range and returning to the pro shop, where I was called to mediate a discussion over times in the starter's book.

I heard her cry out to me, "Hey, Harvey. If golf professionals were regarded as doctors, you would be a country veterinarian."

Judy's Grip

WEST TEXAS GOLFERS have always been known for their strong grips.

Out there where it is flat and windy and the fairways are hard, west Texas players with their strong grips can hit that low tail hook that seems to run forever once the ball bounces on the ground.

They hit some mighty tee balls in west Texas.

But you must remember that their distances are measured in Texas yards.

The same drive that covers three hundred yards in west Texas may go barely two hundred at a course with lush grass fairways, like Winged Foot or Riviera, where a drive is nearly all carry and the rough is thick.

The first thing I did with most of my west Texas pupils was to change their grips.

A Midland girl named Judy Torluemke was taught to play golf at the age of six by her father, Paul. She won the Trans-Miss at age fourteen and was low amateur at the Women's Open the following year.

Judy had, I believe, the strongest grip I have ever seen on a good player. Her left hand was so far over on top of the handle that she had to make an amazingly fast move with her hips to get the clubhead square at the ball, and she bent her spine into a pronounced reverse C.

When she came to me for lessons, her father said, "Harvey, I want you to help her become a better player. But there is one condition. You must never alter her grip. She has the grip of the future."

As a result, Judy and I went straight to the putting green. In all our sessions, we concentrated on her short game.

Judy had led the tour in fairways and greens and was known as a good putter. I wondered what she had come to me for. A friend and frequent playing partner of Judy's confided to me that the problem was that Judy missed a one-foot putt on nearly every round. But I wasn't supposed to mention it to her.

There was nothing I could do to her swing without changing her grip. I worried that because of the especially strong grip, her fast hips and bent spine might cause her problems with her back. But with the suppleness of youth, Judy got herself into position to hit the ball up there with the best.

And not just Texas yards.

Under her maiden name and later under her married name, Judy Rankin won twenty-six professional tournaments and three Vare Trophies, and was the leading money winner at least once.

She did develop back trouble on the tour and had to have surgery, but we'll never know if her grip caused it or if it was simple human frailty.

I get to see a lot of Judy these days—on television. She

has become one of the top network commentators on golf.

Judy's outstanding golfing career is proof that the same grip does not fit everyone.

One champion who did adopt Judy's grip is Paul Azinger, who caddied for Judy on a day when she shot a 63. It has certainly worked for Paul.

I don't know whether I helped Judy sink those one-footers. It's the only time I was ever presented with a one-foot challenge as a teacher.

A Practice Procedure

NEARLY EVERY DAY, I see golfers out there banging away at bucket after bucket of balls, and if I were to ask them what they were doing, they would say, "Why, what does it look like I'm doing, Harvey? I'm practicing."

They are all getting exercise, all right. But few of them are really practicing.

If you stand there and hit balls without purpose long enough, you might start doing it right and eventually find out how to do it wrong.

Let me suggest a practice procedure that I know gets results.

After you have done your stretching, which you should always take time to do, pull out your wedge and hit five full shots with it. Then put it away.

Now use your 7-iron. Hit five shots with it. No matter how good they are, resist the urge to hit more in an effort to "groove it." Chances are you might lose it.

Put your 7-iron aside and take out your 3-wood. Hit five shots with your 3-wood, always aiming at a target. Then put it away.

Now pick up your 7-iron again and hit five more shots with it. Then put it away.

If you feel like it, you may now pull out your driver and hit three or four balls with it. Try your best to hit them good, as though you were on the first tee. But if they are not great drives, forget it. Put your driver away.

You have now hit a few more than twenty full shots.

That's enough full shots for an efficient practice session.

Now take your putter, wedge, and a couple of chipping clubs and go spend the rest of your practice time sharpening your short game. This is where you are going to lower your scores.

Three Games in One

AT A TEACHING seminar, Louise Suggs said golf is three games being played at the same time.

One is the power game. How far can you hit it? In the power game, men have an advantage. Louise called it "the brute part."

Another is the short game, where women are not at a disadvantage. I agree with Louise that in general women may have the edge over men in the short game. It could be that women's fingers are more sensitive than men's. I don't know if that is the reason, but I have seen women amateurs who could chip and putt as well as anyone on either of the professional tours.

It appears to me that once they learn the fundamentals, women bring to the short game a natural grace and a delicacy of touch.

Percy Boomer and other fine teachers have taught the swing to neophyte women golfers by comparing the leg and body movements to a dance step. Women grasp the feeling of dancing better than men do.

The champion Beverly Hanson, winner of both the Amateur and the Open, said, "If you put a hula hoop on a woman, she can learn to use it in a few minutes, but a hula hoop on a man is a hula hoop lost."

After the power game and the short game, Louise said, golf is divided into still a third game, which is in fact eighteen games in one. Louise called this the thinking game.

Each hole is its own game with its own life and its own challenges. Louise said each hole is a world of its own, and she said women are naturally better than men at dealing with one thing at a time.

In Louise's interpretation, women can have an edge over men in two of the three games of golf.

I believe this is true, provided women can put in the necessary time at practice.

Because of physical structure, men will always have the advantage in the power game. But the young women pros today are driving the ball 260 yards and more off the tee, so the capability exists of narrowing the gap, since the golf courses now in place won't grow any longer. Laura Davies can hit it 300 yards off the tee, farther than most men pros. Babe Didrickson considered 270 yards a mediocre drive for her.

Think of this as you are swinging your weighted club twenty-five times a day.

The Card Table— Under and Under

USUALLY I USE a bench for this instruction, but a card table will do just as well.

As an aid to practicing your chip shots, picture in your mind that there is a card table a few feet beyond your swing.

If you can practice with a real card table—or a real bench—so much the better.

Hit your chip shot so that you feel you are going to hit the ball under the bench or card table. You want the ball to be on the ground quickly and rolling in a chip shot.

The Card Table—
Under but Over

THE SAME CARD table can be used to practice the pitch shot.

The difference is that you use a lofted club.

You want to hit the ball high and land it softly. Imagine the card table is a few feet past the end of your swing with a sand wedge. Imagine that you are going to hit the ball beneath the card table with this sand wedge.

What happens? The ball goes high over the table and lands softly. Why? Because you hit down on the ball to drive it under the table, but the loft on the sand wedge made it go up.

If there was a house in front of you, and you wanted to hit the ball over the house, you would use a lofted club like a wedge and picture hitting the ball through a ground-floor window. You hit down and through the ball with a wedge, aiming at the ground-floor window, and the ball goes over the house.

The worst thing you could do would be to hit up on the ball and try to help it over the table or over the house. That is why I say, in a pitch shot, imagine you are hitting the ball beneath the table with a lofted club, and the ball will go up.

Pupils have written to me in confusion over whether I said to use the card table (or the bench) to practice the chip shot or the pitch shot.

My answer is, both.

What you change is the loft of your club and your intention for the shot.

A Fundamental

YOUR HANDS MUST lead your clubhead into contact with the ball on every swing, from the putter through the driver.

On putts and chips, your hands must lead or stay even with the clubhead all the way through the finish of the stroke.

There are as many variations to the swing as there are to individual styles of walking. But in a good swing, this one thing never varies: Your hands lead your clubhead through the downswing.

There was a fellow at River Oaks in Houston who wrote a book about his belief not only that the hands lead the clubhead but that, furthermore, the wrists must never consciously uncock.

The first week Jackson Bradley showed up for work as head pro at River Oaks, this fellow cornered him and said, "Let's get it straight right from the beginning. I know more about the golf swing than you will ever know."

Jackson is a great teacher and doesn't need me to defend him against anyone.

But we all must admit the fellow at River Oaks was

41

onto one solid fundamental of the golf swing that every good teacher and good player agree on:

Your hands always lead your clubhead into contact with the ball on every stroke.

On putts and chips, your hands must lead or stay even with the clubface all the way through. This is a very important thing to remember.

Picking a Putter

YOUR PUTTER IS the most important club in your bag.

If it is your first time for buying a putter, play the field, dance with all of them, and go home with the one you feel most comfortable with.

Some will tell you to select a heavy putter if you play at a course with fast greens, and indeed a heavier putter might sometimes help on slick greens like Oakmont.

But most of putting is mental. You must put fear of failure out of your mind. Let your fingers handle it.

It is a soothing balm for your nerves if you like the looks and feel of the putter in your fingers and hands.

During those spells when your putter quits working, resist the urge to go buy a different putter. Your old familiar putter hasn't really quit working. It is your mind that is avoiding performing for some reason, not your putter. Or as I usually say, "It's not the fiddle, it's the fiddler."

I have known players to get angry and give away favorite putters, and they always regret it later. Punish your putter by hiding it in the closet, if you must, but keep it. The time will come when you will dig it out and find it works again.

A Call in the Night

ON A HOT summer night the telephone rang in our home near the second Austin Country Club, the Riverside Drive layout designed by Perry Maxwell, the place where Betsy Rawls and Betty Jameson and Kathy Whitworth and Betty Hicks and Mary Lena Faulk and Mickey Wright and Babe Didrickson and Betty Dodd and Sandra Palmer and Judy Kimball and Judy Rankin and Betsy Cullen and Judy Bell and many others, as well as men like Tommy Kite and Ben Crenshaw, learned or sharpened their games.

I answered and heard a woman's voice sweetly say, "Harvey, honey, I need help."

I recognized her, a high handicapper from the club. She loved the game. What she lacked in natural talent, she made up for in zest.

"What's the problem?" I asked.

"There are so many sand traps up here." She was playing in a tournament in Temple, Texas, about a hundred miles north of Austin. "They have covered this golf course with sand traps, Harvey. And I am chili dipping

43

with my wedge. With all these traps, a chili dip is the last thing I want to be doing."

I told her, "Grip your sand wedge up at the end of the shaft. This will stop your chili dipping. Hold the club tight with your left little finger and ring finger. If you do this, the clubface will not turn over when it hits the sand.

"This will lead you to hit good sand shots instead of hitting it fat," I said.

"Thank you, honey," she said.

I said, "Which of your assumed names are you playing under this week?"

"I'm Helen Holmes again," she said. "I'll be home tomorrow night. You and the kids be good, you hear?"

"Play well," I said.

Helen Holmes was the girl from Whitesboro who became Mrs. Harvey Penick in 1929.

My wife, the golfer.

A Story by Helen

SOME PEOPLE SAID I used my maiden name when I played in golf tournaments in order to protect Harvey's reputation as a teacher.

But that is not really the reason. I used my maiden name so I could play golf and enjoy myself without drawing attention.

Even when we were very young and newly married, Harvey already was known all over Texas as a wonderful teacher.

At first I would play in tournaments as Helen Penick. I played golf because I love the game and the socializing that goes with it, and I love being outdoors in beautiful surroundings. I could have just as much fun down in the third or fourth flight as the women who were playing in the championship flight, and I brought home lovely trophies like the porcelain figure that stands on our breakfast table.

But the name "Penick" attracted attention and comments that I didn't need. Many women, I felt, were using me to try to get to Harvey. I just wanted to play golf and have a good time with my friends, not talk about Harvey at every tournament.

It wasn't his reputation as a teacher I was protecting, it was my peace of mind.

There is no game on earth like golf to ease a worried mind. For years doctors have sent patients who are troubled or depressed to Harvey for golf lessons. If you get out in the fresh air and compete at golf, it keeps your mind off your problems.

But at my tournaments, strangers would hear the name "Penick" and start pestering me about Harvey, and I got tired of it.

If you want to become a really good golfer, it will eat up your life. That is very worthwhile for those who do it, who have the time and desire to play and practice every day. I had other things to do, like raise two children and do volunteer work for twenty-eight years at St. David's Hospital, and I have always been a devoted bridge player. Bridge is my favorite game of all.

The day I decided to become Helen Holmes at golf tournaments for the rest of my life, I was in the third flight at San Antonio Country Club.

As I left the ninth green on the first round, I was happily talking to my good friend Quo Vadis Burke,

45

wife of the famous teacher Jack Burke Sr. Quo Vadis and I went everywhere together and had more fun than anybody, and I was sharing with her my pleasure at what had happened on the front nine.

A woman was listening to us. She walked over and said, "Is your husband Harvey Penick, the teacher?"

I said, "Yes."

The woman said, "What did you shoot on the front nine?"

"I shot a 48," I told her proudly.

For me breaking 50 at a top course like San Antonio Country Club was an occasion for rejoicing.

"What? A 48?" the woman said disdainfully. "Why, if I had a husband like Harvey Penick, I would be the club champion."

She showed her ignorance of the whole situation. Harvey has always believed that husbands should never teach their wives to play golf, because it strains the marriage. In all the years I played the game, Harvey would never watch me hit balls more than ten minutes before he made up some excuse and went away.

"What does your husband do?" I said.

"My husband is a lawyer."

I said, "I suppose he teaches you how to handle all his court cases. You must be pretty good at it by now."

Quo Vadis laughed, and we left the woman standing there.

From then on, at golf tournaments I was Helen Holmes.

The Picture Show

IF YOU SEE the shot in your mind, your muscles will do their best to make it happen.

One of biggest differences between high-handicap players and good players is the picture show of the mind.

The good player visualizes the shot. Each and every shot. The good player sees in the mind where the ball will fly and how it will land, and thus subconsciously instructs the muscles what is wanted.

The high handicapper probably doesn't make a mental motion picture of any shot. The high handicapper takes a vague sort of aim and whacks away.

Your imagination is an important part of the game. Use it.

Swing Thoughts

WHILE PERFORMING AS starter on the first tee one day, I saw a pupil take her address, waggle her driver a couple of times, freeze over the ball for a bit, waggle some more—and finally step back and look up with a woebegone expression.

"This is awful," she said. "I can't remember what to think about."

She had forgotten her swing thought, the cue that would put her swing into action.

Most likely she had not so much forgotten it as mixed it up with a dozen other swing thoughts in her head, and she couldn't select the one she wanted to use.

Many players use a physical act as a cue.

Kicking in a bit with the right knee is a cue that works for a lot of people. This bit of action is a sort of forward press that also reminds the player to keep the right knee flexed and steady and to turn around it during the swing.

One of the simplest swing thoughts is: Turn and turn. In other words, make your turn backwards and then make your turn all the way forward, and your swing happens in between.

My favorite, as my pupils all know, is to think of swinging a bucket of water. This thought causes a natural forward press that reacts into a smooth, full swing.

Some pupils don't grasp this bucket-of-water thought. As with any physical action, the feeling of swinging a bucket of water is difficult to describe in words to someone who has never done it. The best way to learn it is to get a bucket, put a few inches of water in it—not so much that you make it too heavy—and then take hold of it by the handle and swing it.

There are dozens of thoughts that can cue your swing into action. You will hear and probably try most of them as you continue to play the game.

But let me warn you of this—stick with one thought at a time.

If you have several swing thoughts going through your mind all at once and you are trying to sort them out and select what to use, you will find yourself like that pupil at the first tee I mentioned earlier—unable to remember what it is you want to think about.

Some players tell me they use a backswing thought, a downswing thought, and a follow-through thought. This strikes me as a heavy mental burden to try to carry through a golf swing that lasts less than two seconds.

Don Massengale told me he won the Canadian Open with only one swing thought—to keep his elbows close together at the finish of his follow-through.

So use just one thought or cue to get your swing going.

And always take dead aim. When you are playing well, this may be all you need to think about.

How to Have Both Golf and a Marriage

JUST REMEMBER THAT too much of anything usually causes trouble.

What's Your Hurry?

THERE MAY SOMEWHERE be a good golfer whose backswing is too slow, but that person has not set foot on any golf course I know of in the last ninety years.

There's an old joke that golf hustlers are always on the watch for a player with a fat wallet and a fast backswing.

Bobby Jones said two of the best pieces of advice he ever received from teacher Stewart Maiden are "You don't hit it with your backswing" and "Hit it hard, it'll come down someplace."

I love a slow, smooth takeaway and backswing.

A slow backswing gives you time to make a good turn and stay balanced as you are gathering yourself for the forward blow.

I am not in favor of the pause at the top, which is the only disagreement I have with Tommy Armour. I think a swing must be a swing, and if it comes to a stop partway, it is not a swing.

Of course there is the moment of transition from backward to forward, but the most important part of this is automatically taken care of when you plant your left heel on the ground and your weight shifts to the left.

When you plant that left heel and at the same moment, in a single move, bring your right elbow back to your side—the Magic Move—the transition takes place without your needing to think about it.

Your store up energy going back and release that energy coming forward. Like throwing a punch. Like throwing a baseball. Like serving at tennis.

Some of the top players are fast swingers, backwards and forwards in a blur. This is natural for them. If I tried to make Ben Hogan or Tom Watson or Lanny Wadkins take the club back slowly, I would be crazy.

But in nearly every session I have with Tom Kite and Sandra Palmer, to name two great players who tend to let their backswings get a little too fast for their golfing personalities, I urge them to slow down in the takeaway.

Both Sandra and Tommy always look surprised when I say they have gotten fast. But after they put their minds to it for a few swings, they see the results.

Playing the Breaks

A COMMON FAULT even among better players is getting too clever on the greens.

I received a letter from a woman in Vermont who complained that putting from fairly close to the hole was giving her a fit.

"Every time I play golf, I have at least half a dozen shortish putts that just barely graze the cup," she wrote. "I line up my putts very carefully from behind the ball, as you suggest, and make two practice strokes before I strike the ball. I pay close attention to the speed and try to make the ball die around the cup, so it will have a chance to fall in. And that's what keeps happening— they die around the cup, but they don't fall in.

"I study the break of my short putts quite closely and

always aim so that my putter blade is square to the aiming spot over which I want the ball to roll.

"Why don't my putts go in the hole?"

Without watching her putt, I would have to guess that her putts don't drop because she is aiming to miss.

She is probably using so much finesse in playing the break that she is outwitting herself.

Certainly you want to read the break before you putt. But reading the break and judging the grain are skills that require much practice and experience.

I've had many pupils who painstakingly read the break on a six-footer and then strike a pretty good putt that misses because the reading was wrong.

Sometimes the pupil would say, "Well, at least I missed it on the pro side"—meaning the putt was missed on the high side of the cup, as opposed to the low, or "amateur," side.

Missing on the "pro" side makes the pupil feel better, even though a missed putt costs another stroke, no matter which side it misses on.

Continually burning the whole but missing it on the shorter putts is the result of trying to put too fine a line on things.

I believe that unless you are truly an expert at reading greens, you will be better off to aim your shorter putts to go into the cup, rather than finessing a delicate break.

Instead of playing to slide the ball in from the side of the cup, play to stroke the ball into the front of the hole. Maybe you will aim a shade off the center, but you should be mindful that you are aiming inside the cup, rather than outside it.

If you aim a shorter putt at the cup and concentrate on striking the ball with the sweet spot of the putter, you will make your share.

A steady head is essential. One way to make sure you hold your head still while you putt is to think of seeing the grass beneath the ball as the ball rolls away.

To the woman in Vermont, I would say that she is doing nearly everything the way I like it. She is lining up her putt from behind the ball, and she is making two practice strokes. She is thinking of dying her ball at the hole instead of knocking it two or three feet past. So far, so good.

I believe she needs to think about one more thing. She needs to think not to think too much and go ahead and roll the ball—give it a chance to go in.

Every golfer knows that you seldom miss a four-foot putt that you fearlessly hit one-handed because it has become no longer important to the outcome. Your subconscious takes over and raps the ball into the hole without heeding that infernal jabber from your thinking self.

As Ken Venturi is always saying on television, "Don't give the hole away."

The Best

THE BEST WOMAN player I ever saw with every club in the bag is Mickey Wright. The best man player I ever saw is Jack Nicklaus. Between the two of them, I would choose Mickey as having the better swing.

A Champ and Her Children

SOMETIMES WHEN I have a pupil who says she would love to become a good golfer but doesn't have the time to spend on it because she has children and car pools that demand her attention, I tell her about Mary Ann Morrison.

Mary Ann raised four children while she was winning seventeen state amateur championships. She won the state title nine times in Texas, four in Louisiana and four in Wyoming. She won the Houston city championship twenty-two times.

I asked her how she managed this remarkable feat.

"Well, one thing I did was when it was my day for the car pool, I always carried my clubs in the trunk," she said. "Then, when I dropped the kids off, I would head for the nearest driving range until it was time to pick the kids up again."

I asked if she ever let her kids go along with her at the golf course when she was playing.

"Almost never. That just doesn't work for Mom, and I don't recommend it for the kids, either."

Mary Ann did have a big advantage over women who take up the game after they have started a family. Before she got married, Mary Ann was already a top player.

She was born Mary Ann Villegas in New Orleans and began taking golf lessons from Fred Haas Sr. at the age of twelve. At the age of sixteen, Mary Ann played in the New Orleans Open. On the first day of the tournament, she was matched with Babe Didrickson, Louise Suggs, and Patty Berg. Mary Ann told me she was very nervous for the first few holes, until Babe said, "Oh, honey, loosen your girdle and let it fly!"

At the beginning of her golfing life, Mary Ann did something I wish all women had the opportunity to do. She took lessons for six months before she ever stepped onto a course to play the game.

This way she never had to unlearn the bad habits new players get into when they begin by trying to copy the swings they see on television and obey the tips they receive from husbands or boyfriends.

In 1953, Mary Ann moved to Houston and started taking lessons from Jackson Bradley at River Oaks. She also became Mary Ann Rathmell and began raising a family and winning Texas state championships.

"It took determination," she said. "I assigned myself certain days when I played golf, and nothing short of a catastrophe could change it. I practiced every day. If I couldn't make it to the golf course or to a driving range, I putted on the carpet for at least thirty minutes. In fact, I still putt for at least thirty minutes every day without fail. I think this has probably done more than anything else to help me remain a good player for all these years."

Mary Ann started coming to me for lessons about thirty years ago. Last year I gave her a lesson once a week when she was in Austin. She has been married for eighteen years to Butch Morrison, a 5-handicapper who is a close friend of my son Tinsley. Butch and Mary Ann spend five months a year at their place in Jackson Hole,

Wyoming, and the rest of the time either traveling or at their home at Barton Creek Lakeside, a lovely course on Lake Travis a few miles outside of town.

She told me my two teachings that have helped her game the most over the years are "Take Dead Aim" and "Clip the Tee" (or "Clip the Grass," as the case may be).

"These are thoughts that stay in my mind, because they are not mechanical," she said. "To play good golf, you can't be thinking about mechanical things. You think in pictures. To me, 'Take Dead Aim' means that all I'm thinking of consciously is where the ball is going to land."

Mary Ann believes strongly that all players, but especially women, should take lessons before they attempt the game. She understands few women would have the time or patience to study with a pro for six months as she did as a girl.

"But if a new player could manage to go to a two- or three-day golf school and learn the fundamentals, then it won't be such a shock when she gets out on the course and sees how difficult the game really is. After the golf school, she should start studying one on one with a pro that she likes. It may sound like too much to go through, but, believe me, it is worth it."

One reason Mary Ann loves golf so much is that you can play the game by yourself.

"A lot of people need to have some time alone, and there is no better way to relax than to go out and walk a golf course by yourself."

I treasure the periods I spend with Mary Ann on the practice tee, although some of our sessions are quite short. Frequently, after about fifteen minutes of watching her hit balls, I say, "Okay, that's enough. Now you go out and play."

There was one day, though, when Mary Ann had to put her four kids ahead of a very important golf matter.

In 1973 she was playing as an amateur in an LPGA tournament at Westwood Country Club in Houston. Not figuring this amateur had much of a chance, the scheduler put Mary Ann on the first tee at about 7 A.M. She played her round in a little more than three hours, posted a 71, and went home.

In the afternoon the director phoned and asked Mary Ann to come back. Her 71 was leading the field.

"I can't come back," she told them. "I don't have a baby-sitter."

Half an hour later Kathy Whitworth came in with a 71 to tie for the lead. The next day Mary Ann was on the first tee at 1 P.M. She shot another 71 and was still tied with Kathy at the end of the round.

On Sunday, Mary Ann was placed in the feature group. She went to church early that morning and prayed that she would not embarrass herself. She told me it was the worst pressure she has ever felt in golf.

Mary Ann finished with an 80 and tied for fifth, a fine showing for an amateur with four kids waiting at home.

Kathy won the tournament, by the way.

Mary Ann is one of eight players who represent North America against Europe in the Senior Women's International Matches. She's on the USGA Mid-Amateur Committee and plays in the USGA Seniors every year.

If you'd like to see a good short game, go to one of their tournaments and look at Mary Ann's.

A Golf Tip

As a teacher who is well acquainted with the frailties of the golfing mind, I laughed out loud at what writer Stephen Potter said about golf tips.

He said he was eager for the golfing magazines to appear in his mail each month so that he could clip out the latest golf tips.

"I show them to my opponents," he said.

I know a fellow in Austin, Doug Holloway, who was a high handicapper until about ten years ago, when he went through the golf school that Chuck Cook used to teach at the Hills of Lakeway.

This fellow spent three long days hitting hundreds of balls with Chuck, and within a month was shooting in the 70s. Often a pupil will rapidly improve for a while and then suddenly go backwards, forgetting everything that was taught. But not this fellow, Holloway. Ten years later he is still scoring regularly in the middle 70s.

His secret is that he made notes of everything Chuck taught him and devoutly follows those same teachings to this day. When something goes awry with his game, he goes back to the notes he took from Chuck. This always straightens him out, because he knows for a fact that this teaching works for him.

He has never read a golf tip in a magazine or a golf instructional book since those three days with Chuck. He just keeps doing the same thing, and it keeps working.

Golf tips can be wonderful, but they can also hurt

your game. If an opponent gives you a tip, ignore it.

Preferably with the help of a teacher, once you have found a swing that works for you, stick with it. If it falters, reexamine the basic things that you were doing when you were playing well.

You may find the problem is that a golf tip has gotten into the machinery somewhere and changed your swing for the worse.

The Vital
Long Chip Shot

IF YOU ARE new to the game, you are constantly faced with long chip shots—your ball a yard or so off the green, the pin maybe fifty feet away.

You must learn this shot. It is vital if you hope to lower your scores. As you become a better player, you will still find yourself hitting long chip shots from the fringe. Not as often as when you were a beginner, but you will miss greens and need a good long chip shot to make yourself a par.

One big difference between a scratch player and one with a 15 handicap is that the scratch player will usually chip the ball within two or three feet of the cup and walk away with a par. The higher handicapper will chip to six or eight feet, miss the putt, perhaps miss the next putt, and walk away with a bogey or a double.

As I repeat daily, a golfer who can chip and putt is a match for anybody. A golfer who cannot is a match for nobody.

Learning the chip shot is the best way to start learning the game.

Chipping is not like putting.

Many players, including some good ones, use their putting grips and putting strokes on a long chip shot, which is fine with me as long as they also happen to be using their putter from off the green.

I prefer that you stay with a strong grip, the V's to the right shoulder. Remember that chipping is a little drive, and a drive is a big chip shot.

Many high handicappers want to use a wedge from the edge of the green and try to lob the ball up to the hole, but they do not have the skill for this shot.

On a chip shot, play the ball in about the middle of your stance. Put slightly more weight on your left foot. Many use an open stance, but I don't think it is good for everyone. My own preference is for a square stance.

Grip down on the handle, but stop just short of touching the shaft. People will say to you, "Choke down on it." "Choke" is a word you want to dismiss from your mind.

The backswing and the forward swing should be the same length, as would happen if you were throwing a ball underhanded. A long follow-through tends to come with deceleration, but what you want is acceleration.

Clip the grass with the clubhead when you swing.

Make a couple of practice strokes. This is a shot when you should feel the distance to the hole in your hands and fingers.

Select the chipping club with the flattest blade that will get your ball onto the green and rolling the soonest. A 7-iron is a good all-around chipping club, but there are shots, especially the vital long chips, when you may want a 5-iron or lower.

Remember the fundamental that, in the chip shot, the hands not only must lead the clubhead into contact with the ball; the hands must also stay ahead of—at least even with—the clubhead on the follow-through.

When you practice this shot, chip from different distances. You are nearly always close to the line on a chip; it is the distance you must develop the touch for.

Practice builds confidence, and with confidence you can start getting down in two on those long chip shots.

When you can turn three into two regularly, you will be a sought-after partner.

How Many Wedges?

To THE GOLF pro playing for a living, the wedge is the third-most-important club in the bag behind the putter and the driver.

To the amateur playing for fun or sport, the chipping club is more important than the wedge, because there will be a constant need to get the ball close to the hole from the fringe of the green with a long chip shot.

For a pro, the third wedge with a high amount of loft is often a vital stroke saver.

For the average amateur, the third wedge only adds to confusion over which wedge to hit. Better you should learn to use your sand wedge for most pitch shots.

Get a Feeling Fit

MANY WOMEN START off trying to play golf with clubs that are too long and too heavy and too stiff. They will pluck a club out of the bag of a male friend or relative, take a few whacks at the ball, and the result is pretty well doomed to be unsatisfying.

Other than the pros and lower handicap amateurs, women should use golf clubs that are specifically meant to be used by someone of their size and strength and ability.

In fact, many men should be using clubs that are designed for women. Lighter, shorter, whippier shafts would improve the games of men who are not as powerful and flexible as they think they are.

Women who are new to the game—or women who have been playing awhile but want to lower their handicaps—should make sure that they have clubs that fit their physiques and their temperaments.

It is neither especially costly nor difficult these days to buy clubs that are custom tailored. If you choose to purchase a set off the rack, you have a choice of shafts and lofts, depending on the manufacturer.

Any club pro and most salesmen at the golf stores that are flourishing around the country will help you select the correct clubs, but you must be firm about getting exactly what you want.

The most important thing to consider is how the clubs feel in your hands.

You are the only person who can make this decision. If a pro tells you this new set of clubs is just exactly right for you, but they don't feel right in your hands, then they are not right.

My friend Tom Wishon, the golf club design wizard at Golfsmith, has a number of questions he asks to arrive at what he thinks you want to feel.

He asks, for example, if you want to feel your club a solid piece during the swing, or if you want it to kick, or if you want the feeling of a buggy whip.

With twenty-six questions, Tom can arrive at the feeling you want, but you have to be the judge of the golf club. Be honest with yourself and with the person who is fitting you.

"A feeling is a feeling. You can't really put it into words," Tom says. "How would you describe the feeling 'wet'?"

A set of clubs that feel good, that look good, and that fit your personality are a wonderful tonic for confidence. A confident attitude toward your game means better scores and happy times at the course.

A Matter of Touch

IN MY EARLY years as the pro at Austin Country Club, we used to keep about sixty sets of golf clubs in racks against the wall.

They were clubs that belonged to members.

On rainy days we would sometimes play a little game. For a bet of a dime, I would shut my eyes and someone would pick up a club from a bag and put the club into my hands.

With my eyes closed I would rub my fingers over the clubhead and the shaft and feel the wrapped grip, and I would sink into my memory, and in a few moments I would say, "Why, this is Dr. Miller's mashie." Or, "Yes, this is Mrs. Armstrong's niblick."

I was nearly always right.

There was no trickery to it. Many of those clubs I had made with my own hands. I would shave the wooden shafts down with a piece of glass to get them to the flexibility my member needed. The clubs I hadn't made, I learned well anyway, because it was my responsibility to keep the clubs cleaned and in good repair, so they were often in my hands. Each of these clubs was made for a specific person.

Then along came steel shafts, and manufacturers were able to mass-produce sets of clubs for sale in pro shops and sporting goods stores.

Now it is all the rage once again to have your golf clubs custom made. Rather than just grabbing a set off the shelf, more golfers are being measured for height and length of arm and swing speed, and are buying clubs that are supposed to fit them.

Tour players are constantly fiddling with their clubs, changing shafts, bending the angles, adding or subtracting weight.

Any tour player could walk down the line at a practice range and hit good-looking shots with a wide assortment of clubs chosen from each bag, but only the tour player knows how satisfactory the shots really are. The high handicapper gets more obvious benefit from custom fitting than does the pro, but it's the pro whose clubs always fit.

A rapidly growing number of golfers buy the component parts—shafts, clubheads, and grips—from supply houses or from catalogs and put their clubs together themselves or hire someone to do the assembling. Partly this is a reaction to rising costs; a top line of famous irons today can cost more than a new car did when I was young. Partly it is because custom-made clubs make good sense and are easily available.

I think, also, it is because to put together a golf club with your own hands is a satisfying thing. It is something you never forget.

No More Whiffs

BILL MORETTI, ONE of the game's best teachers, told me how he cured a pupil who came to him with the embarrassing problem of whiffing the ball. She just kept swinging above it.

Pat had been told hundreds of times by her husband to stay down on the ball.

Watching her swing and miss a few times, Bill saw she was making such an effort to stay down that her head dropped a good six inches.

Her problem was not that she wasn't staying down. It

was that the path of her swing and the posture of her body made the club go almost horizontal rather than down and through.

The first correction was in her setup.

Bill had Pat bend from the hips so that her shoulders could move backward and forward beneath her chin. Her grip was changed to hold the handle in her fingers instead of in her palms.

Like most women, she felt uncomfortable and unladylike sticking out her rear end in the proper golfing posture. Bill used a mirror to show her that she looked just fine.

With the handle in her fingers, the clubhead could move along the target line more to knee-high, and then at chest-high the handle could point back to the target line.

With her shoulders now moving under her chin because of the new posture, and the handle moving down the target line, contact with the ball became natural and effortless.

Pat's whiffs were a thing of the past.

They had largely been caused by one of golf's most common and wrongest commandments: "Keep your head down!" It pains me when students come to me with their chins frozen to their chests because they were ordered to swing that way by a man.

Bill taught her a practice drill.

He stuck a tee in the tip of her grip. Pat could then see and feel the tee pointing at the target line in the correct backswing.

Bill told me that she was steadily improving and would become a good player. It was a great joy for Bill to watch her begin hitting proper shots. Like all the top teachers that I know, Bill is in love with golf and gets his biggest thrills seeing his pupils learn and grow.

The Lady in the Bunker

SHE WAS FROM New Jersey, down here in Texas to escape the winter snows, visit her sister and brother-in-law, and use our lovely weather that season to play a lot of golf.

She loved golf, she told me the morning of our session. She loved striding along, breathing deeply out of doors on a course that looked like a well-kept park. She loved the companionship in the game and all the laughs, as well as the cries of despair.

She loved everything about golf, she told me, except one thing, and that one thing she hated.

She hated sand bunkers.

"I know that sheep huddling against the cold wind put bunkers on the old courses in Scotland, but I can't believe golf course designers—all of them men, mind you—are so dumb that they continue to litter their otherwise beautiful courses with little pits full of sand that can ruin the mood of an entire afternoon."

"Why are you afraid of the sand?" I asked.

"I didn't say I am afraid of sand. I said I hate it and think it is stupid to dig holes in a golf course and fill them with sand."

"Let's go over to the bunker and hit a few," I said.

"I came here for a golf lesson, not to be tortured. What shall I start with? My 7-iron?"

"How about your sand wedge?"

"My sister said you told her if she was accurate with her irons, she would avoid the bunkers, which are put there to catch your errant 7-irons," she said, putting her hands on her hips and looking me straight in the eye. She was a classy-looking young woman, attractive, smart. She knew what she wanted, but I knew what she needed. She needed to get over her fear of sand traps. It was silly to let such a simple thing bring grief into a game she loved.

"All right," I said. "Let's see three practice swings with your 7-iron."

She made a swing that was rhythmical and athletic, but the clubhead touched nothing, a loosening-up kind of swing.

"Always aim every practice swing at a point on the ground. Pick out a leaf or a piece of grass, and hit it with the clubhead," I said.

"That makes sense," she said. "Teaches me to focus."

"I don't know about focus, but it teaches you to hit what you are supposed to hit."

"See that leaf?" she said. Whack, she hit it. "See that yellow spot on the grass?" Her clubhead brushed the yellow spot.

I asked her to put a tee in the ground and clip it off.

She did this nicely. Then she dumped a few practice balls in front of her.

"Where shall we start?" she asked.

"We're finished."

She laughed and raked over a ball with her 7-iron and settled into her stance.

I walked away.

"Where are you going?" she called. "You haven't seen me hit a ball yet."

"I've seen your swing. You can play with that swing

anywhere you want to go—Texas, Vermont, New York, California, Florida, that swing will do fine," I said, looking back. "But there are sand bunkers on every course anywhere you might want to go. I can't help your game if you won't play all of it, including the bunkers."

I was almost back to the pro shop before she caught me.

"It's no use," she said. "It's a mental thing with me. I put my feet in the sand and I feel helpless. I chop at the ball half a dozen times before it comes out of that stupid sand."

"You're afraid of the future," I said. "You're afraid of the result of a shot you haven't even hit yet."

She said, "The reason I may be afraid of the future could be well grounded in the experiences I've had in the past."

Meanwhile, we were walking toward the practice bunker.

"It's really very simple to play the ball out of a decent lie in the sand," I said. "There's a system you can use that works. You don't have to think about it. You don't have to fear the future."

She sighed and fetched her sand wedge out of her bag. She stepped into the bunker looking as if she was entering a cold pool of water. Her arms and hands were stiff and tense, and I saw doubt in her frown.

"You have nothing to be embarrassed about," I said. "If this doesn't work, I'll be the one who is embarrassed, because that would mean I'm not able to help you."

"You're not the first teacher I have been to, Harvey. Others have tried."

I asked her to settle her feet in the sand, not too heavy but with a nice purchase. The ball was in the middle of her stance, where it should be played.

"Now lay that sand wedge open before you grip the club. If you grip it first and then lay it open, you haven't done anything except make it harder.

"Square your body to the pin. You see how the club-face is pointed off to the right?"

"Because it's laid open," she said.

"Now tighten your grip with your left pinky and ring fingers. We want the club to go through without turning over when it strikes the sand. This will ensure it.

"Next I want you to move your feet and your body around to the left until the clubface is pointing at the pin.

"Place a little more weight on your left foot than on your right. Glance at the pin to get some feel for distance.

"When you make your swing, make the club come down the line of your shoulders and feet. Make your swing not fast but aggressive . Slide the club through the sand two inches behind the ball. I like to see the sand fly onto the green. Go ahead and do it now, please."

The ball popped out of the bunker and landed about fifteen feet past the flag.

I applauded. She looked stunned.

"You've got it now," I said. "That's all there is to it until you reach a higher level. At your level, think first of all of getting the ball out of the sand and somewhere on the green. You want your next stroke to be with your putter."

"It couldn't be this easy," she said, speaking to herself as much as to me.

"Do it again," I said.

She did it again. This time the ball was twenty-five feet from the hole, but she was as happy as if she had sunk it in one.

70

"I don't believe it. After all this time . . .," she said. "Hey, where are you going again?"

"I'm going to get your bucket of range balls and toss them into the bunker with you. By the time you hit all those balls out of the sand, you will no longer fear your future when you are in there. You may even look forward to it."

"Aren't you going to watch me?"

"If you use this procedure and hit every one of those balls out of the sand, you will be teaching yourself," I said, heading off along the path toward the practice range.

Teaching a pupil to teach herself is one of the dreams of a teacher.

A View from the Window

AT OUR FORMER Austin Country Club location off of Riverside Drive, Helen and I lived in a house that looked out on the twelfth hole, a par three.

While I was tending to business at the club during the day, Helen saw some pretty odd sights through the windows. Two of the oddest were holes in one.

One was by a friend of Helen's who hit a 3-wood off the tee. The ball struck a tree with a loud whack, bounced back into the fairway, bounced again, rolled onto the green, and went into the cup.

The other was by one of our regulars, a French countess.

The countess teed up her ball, took a swing at it, and missed. But the force of her effort caused the ball to fall off the tee. She declared it a unplayable lie and put her ball back on the tee.

This time she knocked it into the hole.

Not for one, though, and not even for a two. Because she had re-teed, the best score she could claim for her hole in one was a par three.

Steady Head

I AM VERY careful when discussing the position of the head in the golf swing, because it is so easy to be misunderstood.

When I say it is all right for the head to move a little bit backward during the swing, so long as the head never moves forward until after the ball is gone, some pupils hear only the words "all right for the head to move."

In no time they are bobbing up and down like turkeys or turning their chins backward and forward as their shoulders turn, and they lunge and swoop and try to locate the ball their swing is supposed to hit.

It is true that all the good players I have ever seen move their heads during their swings, always backwards.

Most good players move their heads even farther backwards an inch or so as the forward swing passes the chin.

The good player's head always stays behind the ball.

Having heard these teachings, a pupil will sometimes nod and remember only, "It's all right for my head to move."

If you put it that way, then, no, it is wrong for your head to move.

You should think about keeping a steady head.

Your head will move anyway, though you probably won't even feel it. But the mental picture of keeping a steady head may be the thought you need if your shots are erratic.

Louise Suggs teaches that the most important feature of the swing is the position of the head. She thinks of her head as the hub on a wagon wheel and her arms as the spokes as the wagon wheel rolls around the hub. If your head, the hub, jerks or tilts or bobs up and down, your spokes will break down or the wheel will come off.

Many fine teachers adopt that same image—to think of your head as the hub around which the swing revolves, and thus to understand that it must be held steady.

I have heard Jack Nicklaus say that his first teacher, Jack Grout, taught him as a youngster to play with a steady head by grasping Jack's hair and holding it during the swing. Grout regarded keeping the head still as a universal, unarguable fundamental in golf.

Bobby Jones said that in his experience the correct swing was performed beneath a head that is "practically stationary." Jones said it is a sound concept to think of the head as the anchor of the swing.

To some pupils, then, I ask that they think of keeping a steady head.

This is totally different advice from "keep your head down." You keep your head somewhat up, and you keep it steady as your swing goes around beneath it.

When I say steady head, I do not mean petrified. I would use the word "practically," as Jones does, were it not that some would take this qualifier as license to move the head forward.

Moving your head forward during a golf swing before the ball is gone is one of the very worst things you can do.

The thought of keeping a steady head is a swing picture that does wonders for many pupils.

Practice at Home

ONE OF THE best ways I know of to practice the full swing can be done at home.

Take three golf tees and a 7-iron and go outside and find a few feet of grass. If you don't have a lawn of any kind but do have a patio or a driveway, you can use an old piece of carpet about a foot square, or else buy a small practice mat at a golf shop or from a catalog.

For this practice, you not only do not need a golf ball, you are much better off without one. Using a golf ball brings anxiety into the picture. This practice drill is free from anxiety.

Stick the three tees into the grass or mat or into tiny holes punched in the piece of carpet.

Swing at the first tee. Knock it into the air or clip it off. Now do the same with the second and then the third. When this is accomplished, prepare three tees again and do it two or three times more, or even four or five, as long as you can pay close attention to what you are doing.

The point of this drill is that it teaches you to hit something with your swing, while at the same time it frees you from the tension of trying to hit a golf ball.

This drill is also a wonderful way to warm up if you arrive late for a round of golf and have no time to chip or putt or hit balls. Go off to the side and stick three tees into the ground and clip them off with practice swings. This instantly notifies your golfing mind that it must get ready to play.

As I say over and over, unless a practice swing is aimed to hit something—in this case, the tee in the ground—it is not really a practice swing, it is merely loosening up the muscles.

If you dwell in an apartment where there is no room to make a full swing with a 7-iron without smashing a lamp or a ceiling fixture, you can still get in a good practice session by using the Slow Motion Swing combined with the Magic Move. Both of these drills are described in detail in my *Little Red Book*. In brief, the Slow Motion Swing is just what it says: You swing the club in extremely slow motion. The Magic Move is bringing your right arm close to your right side and planting your weight on your left foot all in one movement at the start of the downswing. In every case, you must aim your swing at a spot.

These movements can be practiced at home, in your office, or anywhere you have a bit of privacy.

One of my pupils told me she uses a cut-off weighted

75

club that she swings in her private office, and she keeps another club just like it that she swings in her apartment.

Let's remember, too, that you can do yourself a lot of good by practicing your putting indoors on a carpet. Touring professionals have been doing this in hotel rooms for as long as there has been such a thing as a golf tour.

I must emphasize again that a main point of all these home practice drills is to train you to remember to aim at something and then remember to hit it.

Unless you can hit the spot you are aiming at with your 7-iron, the prettiest golf swing in the world won't do you any good.

Practice the Short Ones

PRACTICING YOUR SHORT shots helps in all phases of the game. Practicing long shots only helps the long game.

The shot out of a sand bunker is unique in its requirements and must be practiced above and beyond your other strokes. No other shot in golf prepares you for hitting out of the sand.

You don't need to have a game scheduled to get out and practice your short shots. You don't even need to change clothes. Just grap a chipping club and ball or two and make a pleasantly relaxing hour of it.

The Wright Way

OVER THE YEARS I have used just about every teaching aid you can think of, except for the video camera.

I have no quarrel with those teachers who use video tapes of their pupils' golf swings, it's just that I have never done it.

Years ago, our Women's Golf Association had someone set up a TV camera on the first tee and tape everyone's opening drive in their tournament. At the banquet, the tapes were shown to all. For the next few weeks, women's play at our club fell off 80 percent. Some things are best unseen.

Of all the teaching aids I have used in my career, there are two that I would feel free to recommend to any golfer of any type of build or ability or age.

One is my personal favorite—the weed cutter that you can buy in a hardware store. Clipping grass with the weed cutter is the same motion through the contact area as the golf swing.

The other is the elastic strap that Mickey Wright uses to train her elbows to move together.

It is two loops—one for each arm—and a strap that connects the loops.

The first time I ever saw this sort of thing was on the cover of a golf instruction book that was written more than a hundred years ago. The author, whose name I no longer recall, was pictured with his elbows inserted into a big band of rubber, or perhaps it was a belt. The first player I ever saw use an elbow loop for practice was Abe Mitchell, an Englishman, in the late 1920s. Abe's intention was the same as Mickey Wright's—to keep the elbows moving together throughout the swing.

Mickey was taught to use this device by her early teacher Harry Pressler.

These elastic straps and loops are for sale at most large golf stores.

Anything you can do to make your swing more like Mickey Wright's is bound to be good for you.

Starting Your Swing

USING A SLIGHT forward press, as if you are preparing to swing a bucket of water, is my favorite way to set the golf swing into motion.

I have pupils who say, "All right, Harvey, I'll pretend to be swinging a bucket of water. But then what? What comes after the forward press?"

The simplest way I can put it is to say you start your backswing with your turn away from the ball.

Bobby Jones said the biggest difference between the swing of an expert and that of an ordinary player is the use of the hips and the body.

Stewart Maiden stressed the value of a good hip turn to begin the swing.

Golf being the mental, physical, and sensual game that it is, there are many opinions of how to start the swing. Most high handicappers use a different method every week, which keeps them in constant confusion.

At a PGA seminar, Julius Boros told us, "Start the swing with your left shoulder, and then the hips and knees follow."

One of those two thoughts—starting either with your hips or with your left shoulder—will fit any player.

Try them both, select one, and then stay with it.

In my teaching I combine the two thoughts by saying that the hips are connected with the knee bones and the shoulder bones, and the swing is a chain reaction.

Years ago there was a comic strip called *Mac Divot*— golf tips that ran in the newspapers.

One *Mac Divot* strip, written and drawn in 1968, impressed me as such clear thinking that I clipped it out of the newspaper and put it in my scrapbook.

In this strip that I still refer to, Mac Divot tells a pupil: "Just start the swing by pivoting your hips. Your muscles will recall the subsequent moves. Trust them."

That's as good as any advice I ever heard about how to turn on the motor of your golf swing.

Let's Call Harvey

BETTY JAMESON AND Mary Lena Faulk were playing a practice round before a tournament, and Mary Lena's ball lay several yards short of a flat, hard green.

Mary Lena pulled out a chipping club—I believe it

was a 7-iron—and played a run-up shot onto the green.

"You should have hit a wedge," Betty told her.

"No, the run-up is the correct shot," replied Mary Lena.

"I say it's a pitch with a wedge," said Betty.

They argued for a few minutes. Then Mary Lena said, "I'll tell you how to settle this. When we get back to the clubhouse, we'll call Harvey and ask him."

I should point out here that Betty Jameson is one of the first four women inducted into the LPGA Hall of Fame. She won the Women's Open and two National Amateur championships among her many golfing accomplishments. Mary Lena also won a National Amateur title and several professional tournaments and later became one of the game's most respected teachers.

Both were my pupils. I knew them to be intelligent, knowledgeable, and strong of mind.

Over the telephone they described the situation to me.

"So is it a run-up shot, or is it a wedge?" they asked.

These were the factors to consider: The wind was at Mary Lena's back. Her lie was poor. The green sloped from front to back.

"Without being there to see for myself, I have to agree with Mary Lena. It was a run-up shot," I said.

If the wind had been in her face, and her lie had been good, and the green had been wet or soft and sloped from back to front, the shot would have called for a pitch with a wedge.

I told them, "But when you choose a club, you have to take into account your ability to play the shot. You shouldn't just play the club the book says you should play. Mary Lena felt more comfortable playing the run-up; so, that—combined with these rules of thumb I mentioned—made it the right shot for her. If the shot had been Betty's and she had felt more comfortable pitching the ball, then the wedge would have been called for.

"You are both correct, but in this case Mary Lena may be a little more correct."

"You're certainly being diplomatic," they said.

I said, "No, I'm just lucky to have two such smart friends."

Be Yourself

KATHY WHITWORTH WAS in a slump that made her feel so miserable and frustrated that she left the tour and drove to Austin to see me.

I had been her teacher since Hardy Loudermilk sent her to me as a teenager from New Mexico.

It was obvious in our first few minutes on the practice tee that, since the last time I had seen her, Kathy had shortened her swing so much that she had almost no backswing.

Why would a great player like Kathy have changed her swing? It happens because golfers—even the best of them—are so sensitive to suggestion. Most golfers, in fact, are downright gullible and will listen to advice from almost anyone.

What had happened to Kathy was that when her slump began, other players and teachers started approaching her on the practice tee and offering "cures."

Someone had planted in Kathy's mind that her trouble was caused by picking up the club on the takeaway. She was told to push the club back. Kathy concentrated on pushing the club back, and her swing became short and artificial, and pretty soon her wonderful golf game went away.

"I'm desperate, Harvey," she told me. "I'm not hitting the ball well enough to beat anybody. What am I doing wrong?"

I avoid talking to pupils about what they are doing wrong. I talk about what they are doing right. I could easily have told Kathy that her backswing was too short, but that would have solved nothing. What I needed to discover was why her backswing had become too short. By digging to the cause of the problem, I could fix it with a good dose of medicine that would really make her well instead of just treating the symptoms.

But after three days of watching Kathy hit balls, I hadn't helped her a bit.

It was painful for both of us when she climbed into her car and drove away from Austin to return to the tour.

The night she left, I lay awake thinking about her. When eventually I slept, I dreamed about her.

In the morning while I was shaving, the answer popped into my mind.

I phoned the next tournament and left word for Kathy to call me.

When I heard her anxious voice on the line, I said, "Kathy, when you first came to me as a youngster, you had a natural cock of the wrists at the start of your backswing. That's what is missing from your swing now. You are not being yourself. Go back to cocking that club off at the beginning like you used to."

"You never mentioned a natural early wrist cock to me before," she said.

I never mentioned her footwork or her shoulder turn, either, because there was no need. She did those things well in her own style the first time I ever saw her.

"Forget all those things other people are telling you, and just play golf the way you know how," I said. "You are the one and only Kathy Whitworth. So play golf the way Kathy Whitworth plays."

Kathy won three of the next four tournaments on the tour, simply by returning to being true to herself.

Remain true to what your own inner knowledge says, despite conflicting advice, even if it is well meant. No matter how big you get, always remember it was your fundamentals and your own swing that got you there.

Sandra Palmer phoned me from a tournament after a shaky round. I had heard Sandra had been listening to practice tee advice and was losing the naturalness of her swing.

I told her, "Your muscles are smarter than you think they are. Your muscles will think for themselves if you will let them remember the swing that made you the tour's leading money winner."

The golf swing is largely a matter of trust.

Good Posture

FOR MANY YEARS I have taught golfing posture in the same simple way.

Stand up normally, not rigidly. Make the first small move that you would make if you were about to sit on a high stool, and then look at the ball.

Your feet should be far enough apart to make it easy to shift your weight during your swing. Usually, this is about the width of your shoulders.

I have no other way to teach good golfing posture. That's all there is to it.

Charging Betsy

THE FIRST TIME Betsy Rawls came to see me, she was a nineteen-year-old frosh majoring in physics at the University of Texas. She had been playing golf for two years. Her father, an engineer, was the only person who had ever given her a lesson. The University of Texas didn't have a women's golf team in those days, but Betsy had decided she wanted to keep getting better at the game, and her father chose me as her teacher.

As I have said before, since there was no golf team for Betsy to play for, she went straight into training for the Hall of Fame.

I looked at her grip that first day. She was hooking the ball, which I like to see in a new pupil. I moved her hands a bit, so that her V's pointed toward her right shoulder.

She hit balls for an hour with me watching and making a suggestion here and there.

When it was time for her to go, she asked how much she owed me. I told her, "Oh, I guess about three dollars." Betsy paid me with a smile, and I told her to come back and see me next week.

A week later Betsy returned, and we had our second lesson together.

At the end of the session, she took out her money. "Is it still three dollars?" she asked.

I said, "No, put your money away. You already paid me."

She said, "But that was last week."

I said, "I know, but that was plenty. Three dollars goes a long way with me."

For the next twenty years I gave Betsy lessons and never let her pay me again.

She has said it was the best bargain she ever got in her life.

The way I look at it, I was the one who got the bargain. To have a chance to teach a pupil with the brains and talent and charm of Betsy Rawls is a joy. I feel I have learned more from her than she has from me.

My Banquet Speech

MORE THAN TWENTY years ago I was chosen Teacher of the Year by the Metropolitan Golf Association and was invited to a big, fancy banquet at the Waldorf in New York to accept my award.

I worried for days about my acceptance speech. I wrote it and rewrote it and then rewrote it again. Helen was amused by my labors.

Flying to New York City, we were on the same plane with Texas governor Alan Shivers, a friend and pupil. Helen told him that I must be going to make a powerful speech, considering all the effort I had put into it.

The night of the banquet, Claude Harmon was the first speaker. Claude could get pretty wound up, and he talked for quite a while. Following Claude to the podium came Howard Cosell. Howard had remarks for everyone at the head table and for many in the audience, and this was before he even got into the meat of his speech.

By the time I was called up to the microphone, wearing my white dinner jacket, we had been in that room for hours. I looked out at the crowd and all I said was, "This is mighty humbling. Thank you."

I sat down to cheers and applause from a weary, grateful audience. Sometimes knowing when to shut up is the best thing a teacher can do.

An Outlook on Putting

To SINK A crucial long putt with the tournament on the line, I would select Kathy Whitworth to do the job more often than any other player I have ever seen, and I include the names of Smith, Cotton, Jones, and Crenshaw in my thinking.

Kathy has the outlook on the putting stroke that it is just a smaller version of the full swing and that putting is just another part of the game.

Many players hate putting. It drives them crazy. The very idea of a little putt counting for at least as much as, and probably more than, a lusty drive from the tee is too much to bear.

I know a lot of people would be happy with a game that counted for score the number of fairways and greens hit, and closest to the pin, and entirely left out putting.

But Kathy regards putting as a continuation of what starts with her on the first tee. If she is swinging well, she knows she will putt well.

Kathy practices putting less than any other great player ever did, I would guess. To her, putting is all feel, and if her golfing senses tell her that her swing and her outlook are good, then she avoids the practice green.

However, Kathy is a believer in putting on the carpet

to keep her stroke smooth. We have spent many hours stroking putts on the carpet at the Penick home.

To Kathy the most important thing in putting is to stay steady over the ball. If she misses a putt, she says it is usually because her head has moved, or her eyes may have flicked back and forth with the putter head.

When Kathy was playing at her peak, she said she would get a mental picture of the line of the putt, and her hands would feel the distance and control the stroke, and putting was as simple as pointing her finger.

I always taught letting your putt die at the hole. The never-up-never-in school leads, I believe, to three-putts. By firmly rapping your putts two or three feet past the hole, you put too much strain on your nerves trying to make them coming back.

Betsy Rawls, another great putter, probably three-putted less than any champion. Betsy's putting philosophy was to hit her ball to the hole. As a Phi Beta Kappa in physics, Betsy understood mentally as well as sensuously that if she kept hitting her putts to the hole at the right speed, a good number of them would drop.

Kathy sees putting the same way as Betsy. She strokes her putts to the cup and no farther, knowing the ones that hit the lip will be moving gently enough to fall in.

Her putter is a Walter Hagen Tomboy that Wilson sent her in the early 60s. It's dented and nicked by time, the shaft glued back together after she whacked the ground with it once in frustration.

When I see a pupil constantly changing putters, as if that will automatically help the putting, I like to tell them about Kathy's old Tomboy putter.

With that putter, she won eighty-eight professional tour tournaments, the most of any woman or man in the history of the game.

Mickey Wright has an old cash-in putter with lead tape on the toe and more lead stuck to the heel. Mickey won eighty-two professional tour tournaments with that putter, and she still uses it today.

To me this proves that once you find a putter you like, stay with it through bad times as well as good. If the putts stop dropping for a while, the fault lies in your thinking and your stroke, not in your faithful old putter.

Kathy told me she refused to think of making or missing any putt. In more than twenty years on the tour, she always kept the consequences of every putt out of her mind. Instead, she thought of making a good stroke.

Thin Air

OVER THE YEARS, as a teacher and a player, I have seen many golfers hit shots that flew into trees and somehow emerged on the other side, perhaps without even touching a leaf.

When such a thing happens, the golfer almost always says, "Well, trees are 90 percent air, you know."

My opinion is, if you believe that, you should never play for money.

Consider your ability when deciding whether to play safe or to try to go over or under a tree.

Also consider the type of game you are playing. If it is match play, a risky shot over a tree could cost you the hole but no more than that. If it is medal play, a shot that strikes a tree might cost you several strokes.

The best way to deal with trees is to stay away from them.

Keep At It

SOME OLD PRO many years ago on the links beside the sea back in Scotland made the observation that golf is a simple game, it's just difficult.

Some women who take up the game become disillusioned and frustrated and soon quit playing. Their shots roll instead of fly; their balls bury in the sand; the men in the groups behind are drawing loudly and ominously closer. They don't have time to practice; they don't know how to practice; the courses are crowded and too expensive—and one day they decide to give up on the whole thing.

But if you stay with the game for a while and treat it with the attention it needs, you will discover a great deal of pleasure from each rise in your accomplishments. You will feel the sublime euphoria that comes from the perfect shot that every dub hits once in a while. I think once any golfer has felt that euphoric moment, the game has got you hooked for life.

That is another of the wonders of golf. Not only does it fully engage your curiosity and skills for life, but it is a game that is meant to be played for your whole life. There are many seventy- and eighty-year-old players who are shooting better than their ages these days, and they love and curse the game as passionately as they did as children.

Rather than give up, you should seek good advice from a golf pro, and you should be honest with yourself. Do you really want to play, or is this just a flirtation? If you really want to play, you are in for a lifetime of dedication, pleasure, and, of course, occasional pain.

When I think of giving up, I remember one of the strange things golf did to me in my days as a young head pro. I held the course record at the Austin Country Club of that time—the old pasture in north Austin that had been rolled by mules and chopped by hand to form the first country club west of the Hudson River.

My course record was 60—ten under par. (When visiting a course, both Babe Didrickson and Byron Nelson would ask what was the course record and who held it. If the record was held by the home pro, they were careful not to break it. A gesture of professional courtesy.)

Jimmy Demaret knew I held the record at my own club. But that didn't get in the way of the intense games of syndicates—now called skins—we had on each of his regular visits.

One day Jimmy told me he wanted to show me how he was trying to finish with his elbows out front of his body in his follow-through.

He wanted me to watch his finish while we played syndicates.

Jimmy toured our golf course in 30-29-59.

He broke my record by one shot and at the same time showed me something I love to see in golfers, which is those elbows out in front of the body. I have taught it ever since.

Losing my record stung me a little, to tell the truth. I was the best player in Austin. This was my club. The record should belong to me.

I didn't brood over it, but I did keep the record in mind.

A few days after Jimmy's 59, I turned our front side in 29. A vision came to me: I would shoot another 29 on the back, or maybe even a 28, as well as I was playing, and the record would be mine again forever.

I believe it was that type of thinking, anticipating the future, that brought me sudden disaster. Golf is played one shot at a time. You hit the ball that is in front of you, and you do it right now. The shots that are in the future you leave for the future.

While I was daydreaming about shooting 28 or 29 and gloriously reclaiming my home course record, I woke up and found myself in a greenside bunker at a par-five hole early on the back side.

Without giving the sand shot careful thought, caught up as I was in brilliant things to come, I swung and splatted and left my ball in the bunker.

This returned my thoughts to the moment. But now I was mad at myself. I made another swing, angrily this time, and left my ball in the bunker again.

I lost my temper. I took a full furious swing at the ball and knocked it out of the bunker clean over the green and into the woods.

It crossed my mind to quit right there and walk back to the pro shop.

But I preach to my pupils to stick with it in bad times. So I tromped around the green and into the woods and decided to pull myself together and make a game of it. My lie in the woods was under some leaves, behind a branch, and there was no backswing. I thought to myself: I'll just see how well I can do from here.

I should say now that I urge beginners and high handicappers to pick up their balls in the situation I was in, write down a triple bogey, and go on to the next hole, so as to keep the golfers moving smoothly behind you.

But in this case, I had something to prove to myself. I had to show that I would overcome, or at least outlast, the obstacles that I had created for myself.

Trying my very best on each stroke, I finished that hole from the woods and sank my putt for a thirteen.

When we completed the round and added up the scorecard, I had shot a 70.

A 70 is a good score just about anytime. With a thirteen in it, a 70 is pretty remarkable. The more I thought about it, the happier I became with my 70.

I suppose I would have felt better with a 58 and my record back, but I am not sure.

Golf offers strange and deep and lasting pleasures, and remembering that 70 is one of them for me.

An Aspirin for Sarasota

A PUPIL WRITES from Sarasota, Florida, that she is mystified by the behavior of her 3-wood. At my urging, she has put away her driver and started hitting her 3-wood off the tee. She is happy to discover that not only is she

93

landing her ball in the fairway with regularity, she is hitting it steadily farther and farther as her confidence increases. She is hitting it consistently farther with her 3-wood than what she used to think was a good blow with her driver.

At first she teed up her ball about half an inch. Now she tees it lower and hits it harder.

"I can put the tee practically flush with the ground and hit the ball solid," she writes. "In my mind I know the tee is under there, even if I can't see it, and I feel free to go ahead and make a free swing at the ball.

"I hit a little hook with my 3-wood off the tee, and it gives me more roll for extra distance. I'm very excited. My driver may remain in the closet forever."

Now to her problem.

"Why can't I hit my 3-wood off the fairway? If I could hit it as far off the grass as I can hit it when I know it is resting on a sliver of wood, no par four on my home course would be too long for me. I could even reach a par five in two.

"But I just can't do it. When I hit it off the grass, a good shot is the opposite of my tee ball. It fades instead of the little hook. A shot that is not as good is usually topped. Sometimes, I confess, I hit an outright slice.

"What is wrong here? How can a tiny wooden platform make so much difference?"

First, let's talk about what is right.

Learning to love your 3-wood is right. Stay with it off the tee and you will get more and more confident. Your tee balls will grow steadily longer and more accurate. Keep that driver, because someday you may be ready to use it. But for now, your 3-wood is a hero.

So why can't you hit it off the grass as well as you can off a tee?

I believe you are trying to help it up.

Knowing there is no tee underneath the ball, you are afraid to let the loft on the club do its job.

Tension creeps into your swing. Your clubface strikes the ball at a slightly different angle. Fear fouls up the mechanics you should not be thinking about anyhow.

I avoid telling pupils to hit down on the ball except when this advice is much needed and they understand I do not mean to hit down from the top.

With a fairway wood off the grass, I suggest you think about hitting the ball level. I mean make the bottom of your swing be level with the ground as your clubhead passes through the ball.

Make a practice swing to see where the bottom is, and then picture the grass beneath the ball as you sweep it away with your real swing.

If this proves to be an aspirin and not a cure, here is another aspirin you can try. I have only given it once to one player, but evidently it worked.

It was on the practice tee at the men's big PGA tournament. Don January was having trouble hitting his 4-wood off the ground. You may find it hard to believe that a great player like Don January could be topping his 4-wood, but golf is that kind of game. Some days, something goes away in the game of even the best players, just as some days something visits their games that is magical.

"Got any ideas, Harvey?" Don asked.

I did have an idea. I was trying to decide how to present it to him.

I wanted him to hit the ball level with the ground. The swing Don had that day needed to approach the ball a bit lower.

With an average pupil I would have suggested they

take a practice swing, place the ball where the swing touched the ground, and then try to hit that spot.

But January is one of the top players in history. If I told him to hit that spot, he would hit it every time. What this aspirin called for, I thought, was for him to hit just a tiny bit behind the ball, but on a level with the ground.

"Picture this, Don," I said. "Picture in your mind that your ball is an inch behind where it really is, and then hit it."

"You mean I could just move the ball back an inch?" he asked.

"No, your ball position is just fine," I said. "Just put a picture in your mind that your ball is an inch behind where it really is, and let's see what happens."

He started hitting that 4-wood as good as you would ever want to see. It thrilled me to watch him.

This aspirin fixed him up for the moment, and his genius as a player took it from there.

You might try it in Sarasota. It could give your golfing brain a picture that will be useful and then will sink into your subconscious, and your golfing muscles will hit that 3-wood off the grass the same as they do off the tee.

It will require practice, no matter what you do.

Since you can hit your 3-wood so well off a low tee, there is no reason for you not to hit it just as well off the grass.

Take my aspirin, and then go practice, practice, and practice some more. Hit four 3-woods off the tee, four off the grass; go to something else; come back and hit four 3-woods off the tee and four more off the grass. With practice, you can do it.

Women's Tees

NEARLY EVERY GOLF course has at least two sets of tees for men. There are the championship tees way back, and twenty or so yards ahead are the regular tees for the average players. Many courses have still another set of tees farther ahead, to be used by seniors or high handicappers.

Which tees a man chooses to play from is up to his ego more than his ability in numerous cases.

But women usually have no choice.

The expert and the high handicapper, the senior and the child—all females must use what are called the women's tees on most courses.

For most of golf's history, it didn't matter all that much that all women hit from the same tees.

Unless it had been raining, fairways were dry and hard. We didn't start heavy watering of golf courses until after World War Two. The rough was sparse. The greens were open in front to accept run-up shots and happy bounces. The fairways were fairly free of bunkers in our part of the country, and the courses were not marred by artificial ponds.

A woman could hit her ball down the fairway and proceed advancing it toward the hole at a good clip if she had any ability at all.

But most of the courses that have been built since heavy watering started have been at the behest of real estate developers wanting water and canyons and long forced carries that make beautiful photos in the brochures.

With the watering, the rough grows thick, and many balls are lost. Designers surround the greens with bunkers or heavy rough collars, demanding a target shot.

The playing field is more unequal than ever when women of all abilities and ages are forced to use the same tees.

At Austin Country Club, architect Pete Dye gave us five sets of tees—two for women.

The golds are for championship play. The blues are for our better players who are not at the championship level. The greens are for average golfers. The whites are for both men and women. The reds are for women only.

Women should demand two sets of tees. Not only would it make the game more fun for the higher handicappers, it also would allow the players to move faster.

Refresh Yourself

THE BEST THING to drink on the golf course is water, and lots of it.

If your course is lacking in watering holes, bring a gallon jug from home. On a hot summer day, you get dehydrated in a hurry, even if you can't tell it. Remind yourself to take a few swigs of water every couple of holes.

Avoid those soft drinks that are loaded with sugar. A sugar drink may give you a burst of energy, but it will last a very short while and leave you feeling weaker than before.

The same is true of a candy bar.

Many players on the LPGA tour—like Pat Bradley, Nancy Lopez, and Patty Sheehan—carry with them apples, bananas, sandwiches, and packages of dried fruit. These will keep your energy and your blood sugar up. The new sports health bars that look like candy are advertised to do the same thing, but I never tried one of them.

For years it was popular for golfers to stop at the clubhouse for lunch at the turn. I'm sure this revived some players—and put others to sleep—but there is no way this long, stomach-filling pause could have helped their scores.

The Basic Shot

LEARN ONE BASIC shot that you can hit under pressure and stick with it. If you have a good basic shot, you will rarely ever have to hit a fancy one.

Learning

IT IS EASIER to learn something new than it is to unlearn something that you have been doing wrong for a long time.

This is why it is so important to get started in golf with the proper teaching.

For example, if you have been slicing the ball ever since you began playing the game, and you come to me and ask me to unlearn the slice for you, what I usually do it teach you how to hook the ball instead.

If you had gone to a teacher in the beginning, you would not have developed that slice. Playing golf with a slice prevents you from enjoying the full experience of the game. But the slice is the common shot of the beginner and the occasional player. The anguish of a constant slice drives many newcomers away from the game.

Rather than giving up on what could become a grand, long-lasting experience, turn both hands until your V's point at your right shoulder and learn that Magic Move—bring your right arm to your right ribs on your downswing at the same time you plant your weight on your left heel.

It is easier to teach a beginner to hit a little tail hook than it is to teach the same shot to a player with an ingrained slice.

If you will learn the correct fundamentals at the start, your progress in golf will be much faster and also much more fun.

How Much Is Enough?

DURING THE GREAT Depression of the 1930s, a ticket to a movie was a nickel and hamburgers were six for a quarter.

A golf lesson from Tommy Armour in Boca Raton, Florida, was fifty dollars an hour.

Tommy wouldn't charge anything to his favorites, like Betty Jameson, but to most visitors, the price was fifty dollars.

I asked him how he could get away with charging so much, and Tommy said, "Why, Harvey, it's because I am worth it. Do you think if I wasn't worth it, I would have pupils lined up to see me?"

Tommy used to sit in a chair beneath an umbrella and sip a cold drink if he felt like it while giving a lesson.

"You're probably the second-best teacher in the country, next to me," Tommy said. "Why don't you charge your pupils accordingly?"

I said, "I just can't charge big money for short words."

Tommy laughed. He would laugh today if he heard the high prices charged by some of the fanciest teachers in this country.

My knowledge of economics is weak, but I know that, considering the difference in the prices of goods and services, Tommy's fees of sixty years ago would more than match the modern teachers'. Tommy was ahead of his time.

If you are taking up the game seriously, you don't have to seek out the famous, expensive teachers.

You will find good teachers at many driving ranges, municipal courses, and private clubs.

There are golf schools all over the country. In three days at a golf school, you can learn enough about the fundamentals to start you off toward a lasting relationship with the game.

A word of caution. Some schools teach that there is only one way to swing the club, which is to model on the big-name teacher at the school. In fact, there are countless ways to swing the club, as many ways as there are physiques, talents, and ages of pupils.

If you are having trouble understanding and learning from your teacher, it is not your fault.

Find one who will guide you positively, simply, and as an individual.

Labor Day

WHILE I WAS sitting in my chair one night jotting down words in the little notebooks that I fill up and keep in a couple of shoe boxes, Helen came in from the kitchen. She had been talking to a caller who wanted a lesson.

"It's a man from Springfield, Ohio," Helen said. "He says he and his fiancée are driving down here to see you.

I told them you might not feel like giving them a lesson, and it is a terribly long way to drive just to *look* at you, for heaven's sake."

On Labor Day morning, our phone rang. Helen talked a few minutes and then hung up and said, "Harvey, those people from Springfield, Ohio, are in the neighborhood. I told them the club is too crowded on Labor Day for you even to think about giving any lessons. But they are coming over here to *look* at you."

Helen and I were surprised when they appeared at the door. The person on the phone had sounded like a middle-aged man to Helen, but it was his voice that was old. Himself, he was about twenty, and his fiancée was about the same age.

"We drove straight through," the young woman said. "After we leave here, we have to drive straight back. Both of us are due to be at work tomorrow."

I asked the young woman what her handicap is.

"Oh, I don't play," she said. "I just caddie for him." She clutched the fellow's arm, and he grinned.

"I want you to start playing," I told her. "Pick up that golf club."

She picked it up. I got her hands placed on the club in the strong grip I prefer. The left hand, especially, should be strong in the grip of most women. Look at Nancy Lopez for an example.

Then I corrected the young man's grip, which also was too weak. I showed them the Mythical Perfect Swing and advised them to repeat it over and over in slow motion when they reached home.

I was getting warmed up and was about to begin a putting lesson on the carpet.

But the word "home" set off a bell in the young woman's head.

"Honey, we better get started driving back," she said. "The traffic is going to be terrible."

They thanked me for the lesson and thanked Helen for giving them directions to our house.

As they were hurrying toward the door, Helen asked, "How long does it take to drive to Springfield from here?"

The young woman said, "Oh, we can do it in eleven hours, no problem."

Twenty-two hours of round-trip driving for a thirty-minute indoor lesson may strike you as rather extreme, even for a devoted golfer. But now, on the way back, there were two devoted golfers in the car, one a former caddie; and for this former caddie, that makes their trip worth the time.

She Does It All

BETTY HICKS PROBABLY knows more about the golf swing, and nearly everything else, than anyone I have ever taught or played with.

She grew up in southern California playing golf with Jackson Bradley, and she was already the U.S. Amateur champion before Betsy Rawls suggested she come see me.

Betty was a world-class golfer, but she had a flaw in her swing that she knew about and that was obvious to me. Still, we had the hardest time trying to cure it.

Her left wrist broke down during her swing.

I told her the top of her backswing looked like a cow's tail. She dropped the clubhead at the top. Instead of cocking her wrists on her long swing, she just let the clubhead fall.

What made it worse was her weak left-hand grip. After we strengthened her grip, she started hitting a pulling hook. We spent three days correcting that pulling hook on the range, and then we went out to play golf.

Betty hit her first six drives straight down the middle. Her seventh drive, she pull-hooked it out of bounds. Betty got furious. She stormed around berating herself.

"How long have you been getting angry like that?" I asked her.

She said, "Always. And I don't get over it for three or four holes."

No telling how good a player Betty might have become if it weren't for that temper. But the temper was a result of her being such a perfectionist. Everything she did, she did it well. Betty is an artist and a writer; she teaches people how to fly airplanes; she is a golf coach and a consultant.

One year Betty put out a big-selling cookbook that included Helen's recipe for frozen fruit salad.

I wish she would put out a book that includes the recipe for curing the breaking down of the left wrist. I would be first in line to buy that book.

A Cure for Mary Ann
or Anyone Else

ONE OF MY pupils, Mary Ann Morrison, who has won more state amateur championships than I have fingers to count with, phoned from Houston with a problem.

"Harvey, I'm getting ready to go out and practice to try to stop my left arm from bending at impact. Do you have any suggestions?"

It is perfectly all right, and in many cases desirable, for the left arm to bend in the backswing, but it must never be bent at impact.

A champion like Mary Ann would not be making any kind of sloppy duffer move at the ball. That made my answer simple.

"There are two possible reasons for that bent left arm at impact," I told her. "Either you are standing too close to the ball, or else your head is dropping on your backswing."

Mary Ann phoned back that night and said, "I was standing too close to the ball."

With some pupils, teaching is easy.

The Cactus Patch

PEGGY PRYOR DECIDED two years ago to start playing golf so she would be able to enjoy the game with her husband, Cactus, an old friend and pupil.

"I'll be happy to help," I said. "But I want to warn you one thing. If you ever beat Cactus, he won't like it."

Cactus is a powerful personality, an entertainer on radio and television, one of the funniest masters of ceremony and after-dinner speakers I have ever heard.

For the right price, Cactus will pull one of his best stunts, which is to show up as an after-dinner speaker in disguise—as, for example, the ambassador from Brazil, pretending that he barely knows English. His butchered speeches make his audiences confused and embarrassed at first before finally they break down and howl with laughter.

Cactus is such a convincing impersonator that at one dinner, wearing a monocle and speaking in an accent as the foreign minister from Austria, he asked one of the others at the head table, "I wonder why they didn't get Cactus Pryor to deliver this speech?"

The man told him, "Cactus Pryor died."

Cactus loves golf. He has a healthy ego like most of those show business folks, and he is a very funny and competitive companion on the golf course.

I was giving Peggy lessons right along, and she and Cactus went on a number of golfing trips to Scotland and Ireland and fine courses in this country. They were having a great time enjoying each other and the game.

After two years, Cactus showed up one day and marched over to my cart with a scowl on his face.

"Now you've done it, Harvey," he said. "You have ruined my life."

"What on earth are you talking about?"

"Peggy beat me, that's what! Being with you has made her lucky! She chipped in from off the green several times. She made some long putts. It's got to be all strictly luck."

I said, "Well, Peggy practices pretty hard on her short game. You get lucky when you do that."

Then Cactus started laughing. He wasn't angry. He was proud of Peggy, and he was happy to have a wife who can give him a real game. It's not often that a husband and wife are well matched at golf.

The Left Wrist

PROBABLY THE MOST common fault among high-handicap players is the breaking down of the left wrist. This is also the most difficult fault to cure.

On a full swing, your left forearm or your whole left arm must rotate through the shot. High handicappers usually slap at the ball and flap their left wrists.

You must learn to keep your hands ahead of—or at least even with—the clubhead until the ball is gone.

The first teacher who finds an easy, quick way to cure the left wrist breakdown will become a wealthy person with students waiting in line from here to Hong Kong.

Loft Is Your Friend

ONE OF MY pupils told me during a lesson that she had lost her 2-iron. She remembered having used her 2-iron during a round on a nearby resort course, and she couldn't imagine not having put it back into her bag. But the 2-iron was gone.

"Look at the bright side," I said. "If you were going to lose a club, you lost the right one."

Trying to hit a 2-iron with today's loft is like trying to hit a 1-iron of earlier days.

This pupil has no business using a 2-iron—or a 3-iron or 4-iron, either, for that matter.

She is a once-a-week player with a handicap of 23. Long irons are too difficult for a player at this level.

I suggested that she add a 7-wood and 9-wood to the 1-, 3-, and 5-woods that she already carries, make no attempt to find her 2-iron, and get rid of her 3- and 4-irons.

Why? Because the lofted woods are much easier to hit than long irons.

I asked her to think of her 5-wood as a 2-iron, and to

replace in her mind her 3-iron with a 7-wood and her 4-iron with a 9-wood.

In modern women's lofts, a driver is thirteen degrees, a 3-wood is seventeen, a 5-wood is twenty-one, a 7-wood is twenty-five, and a 9-wood is twenty-nine.

A 7-wood has about the same loft as a 5-iron. But a 7-wood will hit the ball higher and farther with less effort.

Use a good smooth tempo on the lofted fairway woods, and the extra length of the shaft and mass of the head will get the ball up, even with a slower swing.

Loft is your friend. Believe in it and use it.

Strike It

IF YOU ARE having trouble paying attention to what you are doing and thus are not striking the ball solidly, try this:

Imagine that the ball there at your feet is a deadly snake. If it was a deadly snake, you would hit it, and hard.

Quick Cure

AT A TEACHING seminar in St. Louis, some pros called me over to where they were watching a woman hitting iron shots.

"Here's one for you, Harvey," they said. "See what you can do with this one."

The poor woman was scared to death by this time.

"Go on. Hit a ball for Harvey," a pro said.

Her backswing looked like she was waving a flag.

I noted that she hit the ball pretty well. It was just that peculiar backswing that had them laughing at her. I could even picture her conducting an orchestra with her 7-iron as she drew it back.

"Leave us alone for a little while," I asked the other pros.

When they had gone on to other pupils and situations, I asked the woman, "Do you really want to change that backswing?"

"I'd give anything if I didn't do this. I know people talk about me. I feel so silly," she said.

I said, "Let me make a suggestion."

Ten minutes later I called out for the other pros to come take a look.

Her backswing was slow and smooth and rhythmical, as fine as you'd ever like to see.

"What did you do to her?" the pros asked.

"Nothing," I said.

"What did he do?" they asked her.

111

"He just told me to think I am swinging a bucket of water," she said. "I wouldn't wave a bucket of water around like I was waving that golf club. I'd get drenched."

Swing Weights

EXCEPT FOR ENORMOUSLY heavy or unusually light clubs, the swing weight that is correct for the average player depends on how she felt when she got up this morning.

If your clubs feel as if they are swinging heavy today, grip down an inch on the handle, making the swing weight lighter.

Earl's Pearl

MICKEY WRIGHT TOLD me that her amazing run of thirteen victories in thirty-two tour events in 1963 began after an image was put into her mind by Earl Stewart, the fine player and teaching pro at Oak Cliff Country Club in Dallas.

Earl told her: "You mind is a camera. Take a sharp picture of the shot you want to hit. If you take a fuzzy picture, you will hit a fuzzy shot. But take a sharp picture and you will hit a sharp shot."

Skip the Details

How OFTEN HAS this happened to you? You have teed up your ball nicely, just the proper height. You settle into your address position, waggle your club a time or two, glance once again at your target, launch your swing— and it's a disaster. An ugly slice, a monster hook, a pop-up to the infield, something awful.

In the same round, you come upon your ball lying beside a tree, between a couple of rocks, with an almost impossibly narrow opening back to the fairway or toward the green.

Faced with these obstacles, you hit a shot that any touring professional would be proud to claim.

Your comrades will probably cry, "It's a miracle!"

But really, it's the simplest thing in the world.

With the ball on the tee, your mind was full of thoughts of your backswing, your pivot, your grip, your weight transfer, and who knows what else.

With your ball beside the tree between the rocks, all you were thinking about was hitting the ball. You knew very well that unless you hit the ball cleanly, your shot would fail, and you might even break your club.

So you put all the details of your swing out of your mind and applied yourself to hitting the ball.

You concentrated on hitting the ball just as you would concentrate on hitting a nail with a hammer.

Try that sometimes on the tee. Stick your ball on the peg, take dead aim, and then go ahead and hit the ball cleanly and hard without fretting about the countless things that could go wrong.

As Stewart Maiden used to tell his pupils, "Don't worry, your ball will come down someplace."

Ruthe the Champ

MANY YEARS AGO my friend Ruthe Hawkins told her husband that she wanted to learn to play golf. They were living in the town of Gonzalez, about sixty miles from Austin. Gonzalez was at the time the home base of one of Texas's legendary golf pros, Lefty Stackhouse. Lefty became famous for his temper on the golf course. He was known to whack himself in the head with his club and knock himself unconscious after an unsatisfactory shot, or to run full speed at a tree and smash into it with his skull.

But Lefty was a good teacher. Ruthe's husband told her he would buy her ten golf lessons from Lefty Stackhouse. "After ten lessons, if you can break 50 on nine holes, I will pay for all the lessons you want," her husband said.

Ruthe broke 50. When they went to enroll her for more lessons, Lefty told them, "You need to go see Harvey Penick in Austin. He'll put the refinements you need on your game."

Ruthe drove to see me at Austin Country Club. After watching her hit balls for a while, I said, "If you will take lessons steadily for one year and practice, at the end of the year you will be able to break 70."

She made the 120-mile round-trip faithfully every week for a year and, sure enough, shot a 69.

Not long afterwards, she moved to Austin and joined our club, where she has won the club championship ten times—at least once in each of five decades—a remarkable feat.

When Ruthe first came to see me, Lefty had taught her to hit a ball that hooked about twenty yards. I changed her grip and cut her hook down to ten yards.

"This is your shot. Learn to play it," I said.

Ruthe became comfortable with her hook and confident in it, but she complained that she wanted to hit the ball higher.

"Some people hit a low ball. It's your natural shot," I said.

"Yeah, I know what you're going to say next. 'Learn to play it,' " she said.

Ruthe shoots her age or better nearly every time out. Recently she asked me to go to the putting green with her. "My putting is terrible," she said.

I watched her hit a few and said, "You're right. It is."

"What can I do about it?" she asked.

"Move the ball forward two inches in your stance," I said.

She moved the ball forward two inches and sank three putts in a row before I drove away in my cart.

"Where are you going?" she called

"You're a good putter again now. You don't need me anymore," I said.

Ruthe has long been a dear friend of my wife, Helen, and her husband, Hawk, is one of my favorites. For competitive spirit, I would rank Ruthe among my top pupils of all time.

She said I taught her to play golf with a quiet mind.

Big-Chested Women

SOMETIMES A PUPIL will try to use her physical structure as an excuse for a poor swing. But there are great women champions with similar structure, so clearly there is a way around the problem.

I suggest that the left elbow be allowed to bend in the backswing. Make a slow, full backswing, allowing the left heel to rise. Then make a balanced turn all the way through the shot.

Be at ease with the game.

Women's Grips

ALMOST EVERY WOMEN who comes to me is guided into a stronger grip first thing.

I want the left hand particularly strong, with three knuckles showing when you glance down. Make it this strong by moving your hand over, not by rolling your arm inward. Beware that you do not roll your arm. Keep it at ease instead.

With the right hand, I am not quite so insistent. I like the right hand V to point toward the right shoulder, but we may take the privilege of moving the right hand into a weaker position if we are curing a hook.

Everyone who knows me knows what a stickler I am about the grip. As I say, if you have a bad grip, you don't want a good swing.

The interlocking grip is proper for most women because of their small hands. Many of the stronger women players prefer the overlapping grip because of larger or more muscular hands. Sometimes I will urge a woman pupil to abandon her interlocking grip and change to the overlapping if it is a move I think will help her natural swing.

After eighty years of observing women's hands on golf clubs, beginning as a caddie, I believe that just recently I have decided I would change my teaching to women if I could go back to the beginning.

I would put nearly all my women pupils in the so-called ten-finger grip.

I believe now that placing all eight fingers and two thumbs on the handle presents a woman with more power and control.

Some of my pupils, like Cindy Figg-Currier and Alice Ritzman, added yards they needed once we changed their grips to the full-finger. I coaxed Sandra Palmer to try the full-finger grip for more distance. She agreed it seemed to give her power and solid contact, but Sandra didn't trust the grip enough to use it in a tournament.

As I lie in my bed at night and think of past lessons, I find myself wishing I had urged the full-finger grip on many more of my women pupils. I now believe it is the best and most natural grip for a woman to use.

Rolling with Mary Lena

DURING HER DISTINGUISHED career as a teacher at Broadmoor, Mary Lena Faulk developed an effective method of teaching what many consider to be golf's most annoying aspect.

She told me, "I've always thought it shouldn't be called 'putting.' We should call it 'rolling.' What you want to do is roll the ball into the hole."

Mary Lena uses range balls with the stripes down the middle. She teaches pupils to set up with the red stripe aiming at the hole. You know you have made a good stroke if the ball rolls in a straight red line.

"I have always thought I knew a secret about the game, which I liked to share with my pupils," she said. "When it is on the putting green, the ball *wants* to go into the hole. It *wants* to disappear into the cup.

"Keep that in mind when you are rolling the ball into the cup. It *wants* to go in."

Mary Lena suggests doing some practice sessions when you putt—or roll— the ball on the green with your putter in one hand or the other, but only in one hand at a time.

"You can feel which of your hands is the dominant one, and you can put your attention on it."

We remembered a pro named Rod Mundy, who used to hit short putts with his right hand, medium-length putts with his left hand, and long putts with both hands. He won a two-ball tournament with Betsy Rawls as a partner.

Try this mental picture of rolling your ball into the hole. It could be just the image you are seeking.

Remember that the ball *wants* to go in.

Positive Attitude

ALTHOUGH I LIKE Mary Lena's use of "rolling," "putting" is not a dirty word. Putting is half of the game. If you get down on yourself and become convinced you are a bad putter, you will be correct. If you listen to horror stories about chains of three-putts, you will absorb them. I used to tell my good players when they went on the tour to be sure always to eat dinner with good putters.

Use What Fits

MY FRIEND DR. Roger Williams was a world-renowned nutritionist at the University of Texas. I believe Roger was the first person to have the idea that alcoholism could be related to vitamin deficiency or imbalance rather than being a character flaw. But Roger's main thought on vitamins and minerals was that what works for you might not work for someone else. In other words, you might need vitamin C and vitamin A, but someone else might have plenty of those and need vitamin D instead.

This is how I teach golf. The same vitamin is not needed by every pupil.

A Romance

WHEN BYRON NELSON was young, he went to work for a wealthy gentleman named J. K. Wadley in Texarkana at a time when the country club there was one of the best courses in the state.

Mr Wadley was a fine player himself, and he enjoyed becoming the patron of a future champion like Byron.

One day a beautiful young woman came to me to begin taking lessons. She introduced herself as Emily Wadley, daughter of J. K. I figured Byron had sent her to me. Byron has sent me more pupils over the years than anyone else except Betsy Rawls.

Every month, Emily Wadley made the long journey from Texarkana to take lessons from me. I started thinking I must be a real hotshot of a teacher for this beautiful girl to come all the way to Austin with such dedicated regularity.

Then one day she invited me to her wedding, and I realized what had been going on.

Coming to me for lessons was Emily's excuse for getting out of Texarkana to visit her boyfriend, who lived in Austin.

Emily was learning golf, all right. But it was romance that was on her mind.

Post It

NOTHING MOVES FASTER than a good thought disappearing from the mind of a golfer.

Our fine University of Texas champion Justin Leonard, winner of the U.S. Amateur and the NCAA individual among other titles, turned pro and won a lot of money in his first few weeks on the tour.

Then Justin lost confidence in his swing and missed the cut six tournaments in a row.

He went home to Dallas to see his longtime teacher Randy Smith at Royal Oaks. They spent five hours together on the practice tee, not trying to improve Justin's swing but to put it back the way it used to be before he began traveling and competing with the professionals.

As his good old successful thoughts came back, Justin wrote them down on a card. He and his teacher decided on seven good fundamental things for Justin to remember, beginning with his grip.

Justin wrote down seven good thoughts on a card and fastened the card to his yardage book, where he would see them as often as needed.

So you see, you high handicappers are not alone in forgetting the good thoughts you learn at lessons or while making your way around the golf course.

But I doubt if more than a few of you have bothered to write down those good thoughts as you learned them. If you did write them down and kept them within reach, you would improve your handicap and your confidence.

Universal Advice

I ASKED MARY Lena Faulk if, after her long career as a top player and teacher, she could decide on any one piece of advice she would give to all golfers, regardless of sex, physique, age, or ability.

"Yes, I certainly can," she said. "I would tell all golfers to remember the game is played one stroke at a time. Hit the ball that's in front of you, and do your best on every shot. You can't play the next shot until after you have played this one.

"I don't care who you are, you're not going to hit it perfect every time. Do your best with what you've got today, and do it one shot at a time. That's what I would tell every golfer."

A Story by Mickey Wright

WHEN I WAS eleven, my father used to take me with him to the driving range at night. With a cut-down club, I would hit bucket after bucket of balls, and I loved it. For the rest of my life, I have loved to swing a golf club. To me the swing is the ultimate joy in golf and certainly one of the most pleasing things in life. I really didn't play golf for fun. I played golf to be the best woman golfer in the world. For fun, I swung the club.

I still do. Nearly every morning at seven, I step out behind my house alongside a golf course in Florida, and I hit balls for a couple of hours out across the fourteenth and fifteenth fairways. A little before nine, the early birds start arriving at the thirteenth green. I walk out across the fairways and pick up my balls and bring them home to hit tomorrow. I feel refreshed and calm and ready for the day. Hitting golf balls is meditation. It is like running a vacuum cleaner through my mind and removing any bad or annoying thoughts.

I might have remained totally caught up in the aesthetic pleasures of the golf swing to the detriment of actually winning tournaments if not for Betsy Rawls, who told me I was too swing conscious and took me to see her only teacher, Harvey Penick, at Austin Country Club. I was often with Harvey for the next four years, and I moved to Dallas and fell under the wonderful influence of Earl Stewart at Oak Cliff Country Club. Earl wouldn't watch me practice very much. I would ask him to watch me hit balls, and he would say, "No, but I'll meet you on the tee in five minutes, and we'll play golf instead."

When I fell in love with the golf swing at the age of eleven, I was a tall girl, five feet nine, which is my present height. My father, a successful attorney in San Diego, had played football at the University of Michigan. He bought me a baseball glove and bat and ball when I was four and would pitch to me for hours in the backyard. I learned to swing hard and hit the ball hard.

As I got better at the driving range, my father, Arthur,

said I could play golf with him at La Jolla Country Club if I would take lessons from Johnny Bellante, the pro at the club.

Johnny cut a eucalyptus branch into a switch and gave it to me. He said, "Mickey, I want you to swing this switch until you can make it sing."

I learned to make the switch sing its highest note at the bottom of my swing.

It is a wonderful way to learn the swing. Johnny was also the first teacher of Gene Littler, who had his own eucalyptus switch.

Johnny taught me balance and rhythm. After three years with him and one year with Fred Sherman at Mission Valley Country Club, I won the Southern California Junior at San Gabriel Country Club and attracted the attention of the respected teaching pro Harry Pressler.

He introduced himself and offered to teach me. A few days later I phoned, and he drove from Los Angeles to our home in San Diego for dinner and a lesson on the carpet.

We had a big mirror. Harry showed me the positions of the swing. He convinced me, as I still believe today, that there is one prescribed golf swing that is correct and will work for everybody—a teaching that is opposite the teaching of Harvey Penick, Tommy Armour, and some of the other greats. Earl Stewart's swing looked nothing like mine.

But as a youth, I had seen three women California champions who were students of Harry Pressler. All three women had beautiful, balanced, powerful, perfect swings. I wanted to look like those three women, who learned it from Harry Pressler.

Harry taught me to keep the club square throughout the swing. I mean square at address. Square halfway through the backswing. Square the the top of the swing. Square at impact. Square halfway through the finish of the swing.

I am saying that your clubface is square to your body as you turn through the swing. You could stop at each of these positions and put your club down on the ground, and your clubface would be square to your body.

This is a completely different animal from "square to square." Square to square is keeping your clubface square with the ball. To stay square with the ball, your clubface must shut going back and open coming down. This method works very well for some, including some champions, but it has ruined many other golfers.

For two years my mother, Kathryn, drove me 125 miles to Los Angeles every Saturday morning so I could have a lesson from Harry. He placed me in the square positions, and I learned the feeling of them. I learned that for me a swing is a conscious feeling of the weight and position of the clubhead at all times. My knowledge of my swing was so self-absorbing that it was years before I realized I hadn't really learned to play golf.

As a seventeen-year-old psychology major at Stanford, I won the USGA Junior at Monterey Peninsula Country Club. A year later I turned pro and joined the tour driving a secondhand car. I started tampering with my swing, an awful mistake. I kept experimenting. I took lessons from Les Bolstad at the University of Minnesota and from Stan Kertes at Bryn Mawr in Pennsylvania. I kept wanting to be better. I was feeling sorry for myself that I wasn't improving fast enough.

My best friend on tour, Betsy Rawls, won the St. Petersburg Open in 1958. I was happy for her, of course, but I was moping around. Betsy told me, "You'll be better if you quit feeling sorry for yourself. You hit every one of your own shots in this tournament. Nobody took your club and hit one for you. Each shot is your responsibility. Accept it."

That year Betsy took me to see Harvey Penick. Betsy hadn't started playing golf until she was seventeen, but she won ten tournaments in 1957 alone and won four U.S. Opens in her career. I figured Harvey must know what he was talking about.

My first two weeks with Harvey were horribly frustrating.

I had gone to him because I wanted to improve my swing, but he didn't suggest one single change in what I was doing with the club. He just quietly kept telling me how good I was. He would select good points in my swing and compliment them and have me concentrate on them. It was positive reinforcement at all times.

But I was looking for magical swing changes, and what Harvey kept telling me was, "Your swing is wonderful. Now the most important thing is to get the ball into the hole as best you can, in less strokes than it takes your opponents to do it."

All that year, on every single tournament shot, I reminded myself, as both Betsy and Harvey kept saying, "This is your own responsibility. Do it as well as you can. Make no excuses. Take dead aim, and go ahead and do it. Pretty is as pretty does."

I won five tournaments that year, including the U.S. Open and the LPGA.

I had been letting it bother me that I would hit two perfect shots to the green and have two putts for a par, and my playing partner might hit three bad shots and sink a forty-foot putt and make the same score I did. It didn't seem fair.

Earl Stewart taught me the same thing Harvey had

been teaching me, which was to keep the ball in the fairway and put it into the hole in less strokes than the other players took.

I was still in love with the swing, but I wanted to win and be the best, so I had to crank up my competitive level and shoot low scores.

I believe I come closer to striking the ball at the exact bottom of my swing than almost any other good player does. I hit the ball higher with each club than other pros because I hit it with the original loft that is on the club-face. I do this by hitting it square, exactly as in the address position, the way the clubhead was designed to fit on the ground.

Harry Pressler taught me in a very absolute way. It was exactly the opposite from the way Harvey teaches, which is extremely individual. But I think the reason Harvey's students become such good players is that Harvey really understands playing the game. Getting it in the hole in the fewest number of strokes is the way you win the game. Harvey's students have magnificent short games. They have the ability to think the ball around the golf course and get it in no matter what happens. Look at what Tom Kite did in terrible weather on the last round to win the Open at Pebble Beach.

It takes a tremendous amount of maturity to play the way Harvey wanted me to play. When I went to him, I wasn't that mature. I was very much a spoiled brat who thought if you swung it good and hit it good, you ought to score good, and I was having to learn otherwise.

I enjoyed hanging out and listening to Harvey talk and watching him teach. He would use his weed cutter and tell everybody to take dead aim and clip the tee. Judy Kimball and Peggy Wilson and Betsy Cullen and Betsy Rawls and Kathy Whitworth and other good women players were always around. Harvey loved to show off his trick shots. He would have us shout "hook" or "slice" or "low" or "high" in the middle of his swing, and that's how the ball would behave.

One thing about Harvey's teaching that is absolutely outstanding, that takes the patience of Job, which most teachers don't have, is Harvey's ability to teach a really good grip and be a stickler for it. Most pros will tell you the most important thing in golf is your grip, and they spend a few seconds talking about it, and that's the last you hear of it.

But not Harvey. I have never seen one of his students who has a bad grip. I've heard him say many times that a golf swing is determined by the grip, and I believe it.

The thing that started the end of my tournament career was a cyst in my left wrist. There was a slight bone chip in there, too. I literally could not hold on to a golf club. They put me in a cast for six weeks, and my wrist healed enough so that I could come back and play some more, but I had to change my grip a little bit to do it.

I strengthened my grip, but I couldn't swing the club to my satisfaction anymore. Then I developed cysts in my feet that were very painful, and I played in tennis shoes in a tournament later, after I had retired to Florida.

I had realized the time was coming when I would have to leave the tour. I didn't want to say good-bye, so I quit while I was still at the championship level and have played very seldom since.

Maybe if I lived in a compound with other retired professional golfers, I would play more often. But then I would get very competitive, and it would get to be hard work and not much fun. When you try to play golf at the top level, it's work. It's enjoyable work, but it is not fun.

Strumming my guitar was more fun than playing golf. If I could have been anything in life I wished, I would have been a country singer.

But of course, I couldn't sing and I was no genius playing the guitar. I could never do it for a living, but I still do it for fun.

And I start nearly every morning behind my house swinging a golf club and hitting those balls across the golf course while the dew is still on the grass. Right now, I'm working on weight transference. You must move your weight correctly to make a satisfying swing. As the years go by, it gets a little harder to make my legs work right, and I have to think about it. This keeps me from getting hung up in my mind with a bunch of other stuff.

I guess you could say it has come full circle for me. When I was eleven years old, the swing was the thing. Then I went out and won eighty-two tournaments by getting the ball into the hole in less strokes than my competition, and now my swing is the thing again.

When to Offer Golf Advice to Your Spouse

IF HE ASKS.

A Story by
Betsy Rawls

MY FATHER, WHO was quite a good player, took me out for my first round of golf in the spring of my senior year of high school in Arlington, Texas. From the first time I swung a club, I was determined to play the game well. At the time I had no special desire to win tournaments, but I have always had a drive that pushed me to try for perfection, and golf is a game in which perfection stays just out of reach.

A little more than a year after my first round of golf, we moved to Austin, where my brother and I enrolled at the University of Texas. I was a heavy reader and had gone through all of Charles Dickens and Victor Hugo by the time I was sixteen, but math and science were my special interests.

During the time it took for me to graduate Phi Beta Kappa in physics, I spent more hours in the lab than on the golf course. During the summers, though, I put my books aside, practiced hard, and played in as many golf tournaments as I could.

From the beginning of my life in Austin until this very day, Harvey Penick has been my only golf teacher.

Under Harvey's patient guidance, I won the Austin city title, two Texas state championships, the Trans-Mississippi and the Broadmoor Invitation, and finished second to Babe Zaharias in the U.S. Open before the ink was dry on my diploma.

After my last exam at the university in Austin, Betty Dodd and I took off driving to Florida and won the Hollywood Four-Ball by defeating Pat O'Sullivan and Mae Murray in the final. Betty and I made a good team, though our choices of music to listen to on the road could hardly have been more different. I loved opera, especially Wagner. My favorite was *Tristan and Isolde*. Betty soothed her nerves by playing her guitar and singing country tunes.

I was still an amateur until after the Titleholders in Augusta, Georgia, when Wilson Sporting Goods offered me a job that turned me into a professional.

During my pro career I won fifty-five tournaments, including four U.S. Women's Opens, two LPGAs, and two Western Opens in the days when the Western was considered a major.

I retired as a player in 1975 and became LPGA Tournament Director for six years. After leaving that office, I took my present job as executive director for the McDonald's LPGA championship, which is a major. I don't have time to play much golf anymore, and when I do get out on the course I am grateful that as a teenager I was so thoroughly grounded in fundamentals that I have never forgotten how to play.

Harvey uses just as much lesson time as is necessary to aid his pupil. But he never causes a pupil to become fatigued. He knows fatigue stymies learning.

Thumbing through a book on educational psychology, I can find Harvey Penick's methods described and approved on almost every page.

But the true test of his teaching, lesson after lesson, is best summarized in a chapter called "Principles of Sensorimotor Learning." One of the most vital of these principles is that a learning experience should give the student a feeling of satisfaction and reward, and the sensation that a job is being well done.

This is a good description of the feelings I have had after a lifetime of lessons with Harvey Penick, who built my golf swing, bless his giant heart.

Enough Is Enough

BEFORE A FULL shot, one practice swing is enough. If you make two or three practice swings, how do you know which one you will use on the ball?

Learn Etiquette from Barbara

YOU CAN LEARN a grip, stance, and swing at a driving range and enjoy hitting balls every day for the rest of your life.

But before you take your swing to a golf course, there

is something else that you must learn, something vital to your experience of the game.

You must learn the etiquette of golf.

This is different from learning the rules of golf. Most players never learn all the rules, which fortunately are written in a book for quick consultation, but they keep on playing anyhow.

One of my members told me, "We tee the ball up, and then don't touch it until it is on the green. We hole every putt. We know what 'out of bounds' means. What else do we need to know?"

That's a pretty good summation of the rules of golf.

I believe the rules of etiquette were best simplified by the British pro Abe Mitchell when he said it all boils down to thoughtfulness.

If you observe the rules of etiquette and play promptly, you will always be a welcome golfing companion, regardless of your handicap.

How do you learn the rules of etiquette?

My suggestion is to buy and memorize a book called *Golf Etiquette* that is written by my longtime friend and pupil Barbara Puett with help from Jim Apfelbaum.

Barbara's book answers questions you may have never thought to ask. Follow its guidance and you will be popular at the golf course.

She tells you where to stand while a comrade is playing, how to be ready when it is your turn, what to wear on the course, and basic good manners. If you follow Barbara's directions, you will be a popular player whether your game is good or not.

Barbara is now a teaching pro here in Austin, specializing in teaching the game to newcomers. More than half of her classes are women, I am happy to say.

Perceptions

Ben Hogan said when he was hitting the ball at his very purest, his golf clubs felt "little tiny."

He said his clubs felt so light that he was hardly aware of them. And yet, Ben used a very heavy driver with the stiffest shaft I ever saw. I doubt I could even have swung his driver, but to Hogan it was like a feather when he was at the top of his game.

Another Reason to Clip the Tee

Many high handicappers flinch at the moment of impact. They actually slow down, even seem to draw back, and they rear their bodies upright as if trying to escape the confrontation of club and ball.

The simplest way to cure this fault is to clip the tee.

If you make a full free swing and concentrate on knocking the tee out from under the ball, it's impossible for your body to lift up.

I get many letters from pupils and friends who want to know how they can ever give up the crutch of clipping the tee and go to the reality of playing the ball as it lies.

My suggestion is that as you practice clipping the tee with your irons, you gradually lower the tee until it is level with the earth. Just knowing the tee is there will give you confidence. Once you have confidence, you can take it to the course and not need a tee.

But when problems come up, go to the practice range and resume clipping the tee. This will usually set your swing right.

Follow the Line

PAT GAINER WON our club championship the last season we were at our Riverside Drive location. We moved across town to our new Pete Dye layout beside Lake Austin, and Pat was beaten in the final for the next three years.

I had a talk with her one afternoon on the practice tee. I said, "Pat, you are worrying too much about your bad shots. Forget them. Put your best effort on the shot you are facing right now. Stop berating yourself for something that happened in the past. Playing golf is much easier if you have a quiet mind."

She said, "All right, I'll do it. But first take a look at my putting. It's gone all wrong somehow."

We went to the putting green. I changed her stance and grip. She started sinking putts. Later that year, Pat was facing a fifteen-foot breaking putt for a par on the last hole and a round of even par 72, a classy score anytime but especially is the early years, when some of our members were complaining that the new course was too difficult.

Pat studied the putt from behind the ball, made a couple of practice strokes to get the feel for the distance, and then rapped the ball right into the hole.

She told me, "Harvey, something strange and wonderful is happening."

I asked what she was experiencing.

"I see a line to the cup," she said. "When I look at the putt from behind, I see a line about an inch wide, a little darker than the grass, that is the path my ball will take into the hole. I see it most pronounced on breaking putts and most vivid on bright days."

"Where do you think this line comes from?" I asked.

"I believe it comes from having confidence. After our putting lesson, I started putting really well, and all of a sudden this line began to appear on the green. The more I trust it, the more clear the line becomes. It looks almost like a trough that leads into the cup."

Pat has been seeing a line to the cup for about ten years now. I can tell you one thing about it for sure—do not challenge Pat to a putting contest.

Oh yes. Pat has won two more club championships since she began seeing the line.

A Helping Hand from a Legend

JOAN WHITWORTH, ONE of my favorite friends and pupils, took a trip to Fort Worth with her husband, Harry,
a few years ago to play in the couples' tournament at
Shady Oaks Country Club.

They knew Shady Oaks was where Ben Hogan ate
lunch and hit golf balls nearly every day. Joan asked a
member what were her chances of seeing Hogan. She
was told that Ben would play the par threes early in the
morning and hit balls in a secluded place, and then sit at
his regular table in the men's grill, and her chance of
seeing him was slim.

"But you never know," the member said. "Ben sits at
a table beside a big window so he can see players in
action. Directly below his vantage point is a practice bunker.

"One morning last week, a woman was in the practice
bunker having a horrible time. She was a high handicapper who was totally frustrated. She kept whacking
away, but she couldn't hit the ball out of the bunker.

"I don't know how long Hogan might have sat up
there at his table watching the woman in the bunker, but
her failures must have disturbed him for her sake and
maybe for his. How could Ben enjoy his lunch, watching
such a performance? Or maybe his heart went out to
her. Who knows?

"Suddenly Hogan walked out of the clubhouse and went to the woman in the bunker. He stepped in beside her and began giving her a lesson. Within a few minutes, she was clipping her balls out of the bunker just like some expert. Hogan went back inside to finish his lunch. I'd give anything to know what he told her, but I guess I never will."

I can imagine Ben being moved to share his knowledge with the woman. I knew him and played golf with him long before he became a legend. He could be a warm and charming fellow, and as a young pro he was a terrific salesman for the game at clinics and exhibitions.

Exercise

PEOPLE WHO SAY playing golf is not exercise have never been caddies.

Also, people who sneer at the amount of physical effort required in a round of golf are people who don't play golf or people who define exercise as running a marathon.

A full golf swing uses nearly every muscle in the body.

The head bone is connected to the neck bone, and so forth, on down to the bottom of the feet, and almost every connection is called upon to perform in the hitting of a golf ball.

There definitely are golf muscles that must be developed if you are to hit the ball far and with authority, but even the weakest swing uses the feet, the legs, the hips, the shoulders, the arms and hands.

If you walk eighteen holes around the course, give yourself credit for a brisk stroll of five or six miles. If you carry your own bag or pull it in a trolley, give yourself a little extra credit on your calorie-burning chart.

Even if you ride in a golf car, you will put in a couple of miles standing and moving on your feet that I would call exercise.

Scientists have figured out that a full swing with a driver by a good player uses about four horsepower of energy.

The full swing of a good player may look effortless and relaxed. But take a closer look at the player's face at the moment of impact. What you will see is anything but relaxation. The concentration is intense, the lips are tight, the teeth are gritted. The point of power is in the moment.

What you want in the golf swing is, as Jack Burke said, a feeling of controlled violence.

This definitely equates to exercise.

If you come home after a round and your mate says, "What you are tired for? All you did was play golf," I don't know how you can explain it or if you should even try. It's like trying to explain music to someone with a tin ear.

Betsy Rawls understood in her early days as a pupil and player that physical condition is very important to a golfer. Betsy got her sleep and ate a good diet, and the last six holes of nearly every match belonged to her.

In my opinion, playing golf is a fine way to exercise. Not only do you use your muscles, you use your mind. A good round of golf leaves you pleasantly satisfied physically, mentally, and emotionally.

Listen to the Swish

To UNDERSTAND WHAT clubhead speed means, turn your golf club upside down and grip it just below the clubhead and swing it hard and listen to the swishing sound it makes.

The swish is where the fastest part of your swing is.

You should hear the swish right at the ball.

If you hear the swish early in your downswing, you are hitting from the top. Keep swinging until your swish is in the right place.

This sounds almost comical, but if I shorten your swing, your swish is going to be someplace different than it was when your swing was longer.

You have to concentrate on getting the maximum speed where the ball is. Listen to your swish to find out where you are.

There is no rule that says every practice swing on the golf course has to be the normal one with your clubface brushing the grass. Turn your club upside down and swish it a few times to find the feeling of speed and power.

Even when you are taking an upside-down practice swing, aim the butt of your club at a target on the ground and give it a healthy swish.

Divots

―――――

FROM A PUPIL'S divot—how deep it is, the direction it is going, the shape of it—I learn a lot.

It is best if I can see the ball, too. For instance, if the divot is cut across from right to left, and the ball goes to the right, I know the pupil is swinging from outside toward inside. If the divot is the same but the ball goes to the left, I know the clubface is closed.

You can close a clubface as much as possible and make a swing, and the divot is still going to indicate the path of the club, not the angle of the face.

Many of the top pros play a fade as their regular shot, believing a fade is easier to control. Their divots go from right to left. On a high handicapper, this divot would mean a slice or a pull hook.

I like for my pupils to show me a divot that is thin and shallow and straight down the line.

Dropped at the Top

―――――

MANY WOMEN PUPILS reach the top of their backswing and then drop the club. I don't mean literally drop it on the ground. What they do is loosen their grip at the top

142

and allow the clubhead to dip below horizontal, sometimes far below.

This is not necessarily bad.

One of my playing pupils, Theo Windsor, drops her club so far below horizontal on her backswing that the shaft hits her on the left shoulder. Then, when she swings forward, the shaft will go all the way around and hit her on the right shoulder in her follow-through. She wears out a few shafts that way, but she enjoys a good game of golf.

Bobby Jones used to swing below horizontal going back. He would slightly loosen his grip with the last two fingers of his left hand, and when he tightened his grip again, it put extra snap into his forward blow.

Marlene Bauer took the club as far back as John Daley does, and she had a long, successful career on the women's tour.

I do not advocate this length of a backswing, but I do say good golf can be played this way.

With a long backswing, the one thing you think you should do is the one thing you should not do: You should not hold your club tighter during a long backswing, thinking this will give you control. The tighter you hold your club, the more likely it is that your swing will break down somewhere along the way.

You Want Straight or You Want Far?

OBVIOUSLY, ALL PUPILS want to hit the ball both straight and far. I think the best way to accomplish this is to begin with the far and then later learn the straight.

I do stress accuracy and keeping the ball in the fairway, but I remember my brother Tom, a pro and a long hitter, always used to say, "I'd rather be hitting a wedge out of the rough than, back there in the fairway, hitting 5-irons at the greens with the rest of the guys."

I teach my pupils to hit the ball solid and hard first, and we will worry about alignment once they can hit it far enough for alignment to be important.

Alignment

TO LINE UP a shot, I suggest you stand a few paces behind the ball and draw a picture in your mind of the line that runs from you through the ball and on to the target that you select. Make it a specific target. From the tee, aim at a certain spot of grass on the fairway rather than aiming just generally down one side or the other. Approaching the green, aim at exactly where you want your ball to drop, instead of merely aiming at the whole green.

Approach your ball from the rear and then turn to face it. Put the bottom of your blade at a right angle to the line. You neither close your blade nor open it.

Now take a small step sideways toward the target with your front foot, then a bigger step back with your rear foot. This places your ball a little to the left of center in your stance.

Take another glance toward your target and, without wasting time for more than a waggle, go ahead and hit the ball while the picture is still clear in your mind.

Almost every good player lines up and fires pretty much this way.

On the practice tee, if you wish to check your alignment, place a club across your thighs. Where the club points is the direction you are aiming. This works on the golf course as well as on the practice tee, but it looks amateurish to do it while you are playing.

Sometimes, when a pupil asks where she is aimed, I answer her, "Hit a solid shot and it will tell us."

Watch Your Step

How MANY TIMES have you seen this happen? One of your playing comrades steps off the distance from the 150-yard marker to her ball in the fairway. She takes eighteen steps. "I'm 132 yards from the middle of the green," she says.

She pulls out her 132-yard club and hits an okay shot with it.

The ball drops into the front bunker.

It is often the case that average golfers use their best shots with each club to judge how far they hit it. Hence, an okay shot is not quite enough to carry the bunker. Average golfers usually underclub, even when facing a pond or bunker as an obstacle. If they would use more club, they wouldn't need to see me as often.

But maybe that's not what happened to your comrade.

Perhaps the eighteen steps your comrade took were each just thirty inches long. Half a foot short of a yard. This means your comrade was not 132 yards from the green but 135 yards. Those extra three yards combined with the okay shot to dump her ball into the bunker.

Learn how long your step really is, or else learn how long a one-yard stride is. Really being confident of the distance to the green, rather than feeling sort of halfway confident, is a great reliever of tension.

Confidence

WHISTLING IN THE dark is not the answer. Making big talk might shake up your opponent, but it is an unreliable way to build up your confidence.

Confidence comes from hitting enough good shots that you know you can do it again. You can only get confidence in your putting by making a lot of putts. Yes, this means practice.

Faith is in your heart. Confidence is in your mind as well as your heart. In golf, true confidence will always beat blind faith.

Advice from JoAnne

SANDRA PALMER TOLD me she was rushing to prepare for their playoff for the U.S. Open championship when she was calmed down a bit by advice from her opponent. JoAnne Carner told her, "Never hurry when it counts."

JoAnne does something in practice that I wish I would see my pupils doing. She will hit balls from deep, rough, shallow rough, from behind trees, from hardpan lies.

Practicing trouble shots pays off on the golf course.

With my best-playing pupils, I will ask them to empty their bucket of practice balls in a scattering fashion. Then I will ask them to hit each ball as it lies on the ground. This is preparation for the way the ball will be found on the golf course.

On a practice range you are usually hitting from a good lie toward a field as wide as a football field is long. Players need to practice in a way that accommodates the reality of golf, where this space is broken into uneven passages of rewards and punishments.

But We're Not Robots

PUPILS TELL ME they want to learn a swing they can repeat every time. "Like watching that Ben Hogan playing at Colonial," they will say. "He hits the ball the same way every time. He's a robot. That's how I want to be."

But if you asked Hogan how many of those swings he made at Colonial that day were just exactly alike, I imagine he would tell you none. If you asked how many of the shots out of the seventy that made up his round would satisfy him as being purely struck, he would probably say four or five.

To have a repeating swing is the goal of pupils who aspire to be good or better players.

This is as it should be. Yet we understand that the

flowing of thought and movement that cause the swing is always different in some way from that of the swing preceding it.

One reason is that in golf we never have the same shot twice. You may have played a hole a thousand times, but you will never have exactly the same lie, the same grass, the same breeze, the same temperature and humidity, the same energy, the same vision, the same blood sugar level, the same distance to the pin, the same unrepaired divot unseen on the green, and be exactly the same age—all these things come together in different combinations and prevent any two shots from being exactly the same.

Thus we adapt a swing that is constantly changing in tiny, unnoticed ways to the demands of a shot that we have never actually hit before.

And when something really strange happens to the shot, good or bad, we say, "That's golf." Because how else could we explain it? Robots can perform some aspects of the game, but it requires the human mind to complete the package.

Like a Violin

BETSY RAWLS SENT Mary Lena Faulk to see me for the first time after they both lost their opening matches at the National Amateur at Merion. Betsy phoned and told me her friend from Georgia was feeling kind of low and asked if I could perk her up.

Mary Lena found her way to Texas. I watched her hit a few balls, and then we sat down and talked about her grip for forty-five minutes.

I said, "I know you're from south Georgia, where the people are big and strong through the shoulders and don't use everything they've got in their hands when they hit the ball. I want you to use your hands."

Mary Lena gripped the club with her right forefinger hanging off the handle. I have seen some good golf played by people using a grip like that, but I do not advise it. We tucked her right forefinger back on the handle where I like to see it.

A lot of women aren't very strong in their hands, and they turn loose of the club, especially at the top of the backswing. Women are more flexible than men. With men, there often is a problem making a good shoulder turn. Women seldom have this problem, but they are so flexible that they're inclined to let everything go backward too far. I put Mary Lena in a firm three-knuckle grip that gave her more power.

A teacher has to be careful with this. Many women will take a strong grip and then clutch the club tightly, hunch their shoulders, poke that left arm way out in front, and first thing you know they can't swing the club freely.

Mary Lena became the most accurate pro on tour from a distance of about 160 to 175 yards.

The reason was her 5-wood, and later her 6-wood. She abandoned her long irons and learned to play her 5-wood like a violin.

She told me she probably made more birdies by hitting the ball close to the hole from 170 yards with her 5-wood than she ever did with a wedge from much nearer. She could go up and down the scale with her 5-wood, hit it low or high, soft or hard.

When she added a 6-wood to her bag, that took care of the 160-yard shots that she had been hitting soft with her 5-wood.

Mary Lena and I recommend that women put away their 2- and 3-irons and maybe their 4-irons as well, and replace them with 5-, 7-, and 9-woods.

Why should you work so hard trying to get a long iron into the air when a lofted wood will do it much easier?

Take a tip from Mary Lena and learn to play your 5-wood like a violin. You will love the music you hear from your comrades when they start singing out, "Good shot!"

Home

WHAT A BEAUTIFUL place a golf course is. From the meanest country pasture to the Pebble Beaches and St. Andrews of the world, a golf course is to me a holy ground. I feel God in the trees and grass and flowers, in the rabbits and the birds and the squirrels, in the sky and the water. I feel that I am home.

About
Betty Jameson

BETTY JAMESON told me she always had acute peripheral vision. She could see things happening to either side that the normal person could not see.

This enhanced vision caused problems on the golf course. She would see people moving where they didn't think she could see them. Her disposition was to wait until they settled down. She did a lot of waggling of the club not only for feel and to take dead aim but also to give the gallery a chance to stand still.

Sometimes she would straighten up and step back from the ball and direct people in the gallery to stand somewhere else so she could concentrate on her shot.

On the final green at the Jacksonville Open one year, Betty was playing with Patty Berg and Babe Didrickson Zaharias, who finished first and second in the tournament. Betty would line up her putt and address the ball, and someone around the green would move.

Finally Babe said, "I'll handle this for you, Betty."

Babe walked into the gallery waving her arms and shouting, "You people on the left, move farther over. You people on the right, you give her some room, too. And all of you stand still. Can't you see that Betty is trying to putt?"

Babe had a real talent for breaking tension and making everyone laugh. I still chuckle when I remember the story of that day in Jacksonville.

As a painter and an artist, Betty said she found the most exciting part of life is looking and seeing, and so her peripheral vision has been a blessing.

It truly forced her to take dead aim. We talk about what the target is in golf, but there are two targets—the ball and where we are going to hit it. That's the same in baseball, but in baseball you don't think of hitting the ball to an exact little spot the size of a cup.

If you're good at concentrating in golf and you understand what taking dead aim means, you forget about the technique of your swing and just trust it to happen.

Obviously, it really helps to have a good swing so you know your trust is well founded.

With Betty I dwelt on knowing where the bottom of her swing is. Striking the ball at the bottom of your swing is an art only the best ever learn.

To aim, Betty doesn't hold with the school of picking out a spot in front of the ball and lining up over that spot. She starts with a square clubface and then works from her target back to the waggling of the club and getting her thoughts oriented. It is telescoping, Betty said, almost like in Cézanne's paintings. Cézanne didn't think of that mountain as being way over there. He brought it right up to him. It's a wonderful experience that Betty learned to duplicate.

As a child in Dallas she loved tennis. She saw great golfers like Helen Hicks and Glenna Collett Vare and Bobby Jones on the newsreels at the movies, and she liked the game they were playing, but she probably would have become a tennis player if she had owned a net. Her grandmother lived near a public tennis court, but you had to bring your own net. Tennis wasn't much fun without a net.

Her father was a newspaperman who started on the *Tulsa World* and moved to the *Dallas Times-Herald.* He loved golf, and Betty used his sticks to hit the ball around in the yard, but her was left-handed and she had to hold the clubface upside down.

She would go out to Tenison Park to wait on her dad, and hang around the putting green. She caught the golfing fever. One day around Thanksgiving, her mother gave her a dollar. She went to the golf course, rented a set of clubs, and paid the green fee, not realizing that her dad had a free pass because of his newspaper job.

She played nine holes by herself without ever having been to a driving range or really taking a full swing at a ball. When she got to the tenth tee, there was a fireman standing there on his day off. He said, "Young lady, would you like to join me?" She just hit along with him, and he kept score. He asked what she shot on the front nine, and she told him as best she could remember. At the end of the round, he gave her the scorecard and said, "Take this home and show your parents."

She had shot about 120, but she was hooked on golf. She told her parents she wanted a set of clubs for Christmas. Her father's golf partner was getting a set of the new steel shafts, so they cut down his hickory-shafted irons and left them for her under the Christmas tree along with a couple of steel-shafted woods.

She was a golfer from then on. The following summer she shot a 39 at Oak Grove. She had just turned twelve years old. The *Times-Herald* ran a photo of her swinging a club. Harry McCommas, a wonderful man, owned a driving range on Mockingbird Lane, where she would go watch the ball-striking contests that featured some great players like Ben Hogan and Byron Nelson and Reynolds Smith and Gus Moreland and Spec Goldman. Harry had contests for pros and amateurs. The lack of television or air-conditioning ment good crowds on hot evenings.

One night after Betty had hit balls in a contest, a man came over and introduced himself. "I'm Francis Scheider, the pro at Brook Hollow Golf Club. I would like to give you some golf lessons." She didn't know exactly where Brook Hollow was—it is one of the hidden jewels among the country's courses—but they made an appointment for Saturday morning.

Betty was living in Oak Cliff, south of town. She rode a streetcar and transferred to a bus, carrying her golf clubs. The bus went past the airport at Love Field and past Brook Hollow, but she didn't know how to get off. Finally she went to the driver and asked him to let her off and tell her how to find the golf course. She walked back to Brook Hollow, where Francis was waiting.

They had a lesson and then played a few holes. Betty didn't take golf instruction lightly. She listened to every word he said and watched every move he made. She was a good mimic. More than twenty-five years later, after Francis retired to Palm Beach, Mary Lena Faulk and Betty played a round of golf with him in Florida. He pulled his own cart and looked as neat and sharp as in his days at Brook Hollow, where he had the first carpeted golf shop in the Southwest. After the round, Mary Lena said to Betty, "Do you realize you swing just like he does? You must have copied him as a child."

Betty was very serious about learning the game, and results came quickly. She won the Texas Publinks when she was thirteen and the Southern Amateur at the age of fifteen.

While she was still in high school, her family moved to San Antonio, and her father went to work for a newspaper there. Betty began taking lessons from Tod Menefee at Brackenridge Park, the oldest city-owned golf course in Texas. She and Tod remained close for many years. Tod became pro at San Antonio Country Club, where Betty was given a membership. At San Antonio Country Club, she heard some women talking about this teacher in Austin named Harvey Penick. A group of women drove from San Antonio regularly to take lessons from me. Even on the coldest days they wouldn't miss coming to see me. They were always talking about our lessons, and Betty liked what she was hearing. So she hitched a ride to Austin with one of them, and that's how we met in 1937. She enrolled at the University of Texas and kept studying with me. Helen would drive over to the dormitory and pick her up and then deliver her back to the campus when we were through.

The two most important things I tried to teach Betty were to take dead aim and to locate the bottom of her swing. Ball position must be dictated by the bottom of your swing, not vice versa. Putting those pieces of knowledge together made her a better player and gave her tremendous confidence. Betty felt she could beat anyone.

She kept improving. She won the National Amateur in 1939 and again in 1940.

Shortly before she won the Publinks, she was in Bill Strawn's golf shop in Wichita Falls, looking through some secondhand putters in a barrel. She found a beautiful hickory-shafted putter that looked somewhat like Bobby Jones's famous Calamity Jane. This putter had a little shorter blade and not as much gooseneck, but it had some loft on it, as Calamity Jane had. The putter was called a Spalding Gold Medal. It was sort of rusty. She was scraping away at the blade, trying to read what was written on it. She saw the letters A-R-T.

She asked Mr. Strawn, "What does A-R-T mean?"

He said, "It means art. That's what putting is—art." She bought the putter and won the Wichita Falls match-play tournament with it.

A woman she met in Dallas, Peggy Chandler, had a profound influence on her love for cultural things. Peggy was a very good golfer, but she practically got Betty up against the wall and shook her and told her not to be just a golfer but to widen her view of the world.

The Francis Scheider swing that she imitated was compact, with a perfect center of gravity. Francis was stocky and strong and never shot over 70 at Brook Hollow. He rarely practiced. He had a swing that was just back and forth, back and forth. I don't know any swing I can compare it to, except to Betty's, of course.

Betty really didn't remember golf holes or golf shots and not even tournaments all that well. She was just into the swing. The swing was and is the most important thing to her. It is a fascinating subject that we never tire of.

I didn't try to change her swing. I devoted myself to making her a better player, always with positive reinforcement.

I would make little adjustments, but I would never tell her what she had been doing was wrong. I tried to make her feel good about herself, and so did Helen.

Betty turned professional after World War Two and was a founder and charter member of the LPGA. She won the U.S. Open, and won the Western Open twice. But one of the best things for her was that during all the travel involved, she got to visit museums everywhere she went.

Museums are where you learn about painting. Betty always said that painters are more or less self-taught. They learn by studying the great works, just as golfers learn at tournaments by studying the great players. You cannot go into a museum and come out unmoved she said, it changes you, enlivens your life and your vision. It helps you to see nature afresh. It helps us know we are alive.

I think the golf swing ties into all of this somehow. It is visual, has texture, has emotion, has power.

If Betty were an active player today, she would be fiddling with all this new equipment.

She was at Spalding, fiddling with clubs, when she lost her favorite A-R-T putter. She put it down in the corner of an office, and it was gone. She still rues the day.

But she did get something special out of one of her fiddling trips. She got a very special driver. It wasn't a deepface driver like the one she had been playing around with. The face was rather shallow, and she persuaded the people at Spalding to put a bulge out toward the toe. She enjoyed drawing the ball, and figured if she had that sweet spot forward of center, toward the toe, it would be just right for her. That driver served her well.

I've seen a picture of her swinging that driver. At the top of her backswing, I could see the shaft bending about eight or ten inches from the clubhead, and I knew she could really control that club because the shaft was stiff with just a little give toward the head.

Another thing that was important to Betty was golf shoes.

Bobby Jones wore the moccasin-type sole, and he used to talk about being able to walk up onto the green and feel the undulations with the bottoms of his feet. He said sometimes he could even feel which way the grain was growing.

Footwork is important, and your feet need to feel lively. Glenna Collett and Bobby Jones were both very balletic in their movements, but there was no toe dancing, in that they did not move all over the place. You know, a dancer has to stay very still at times. And there is Tommy Armour's strong statement: He would say, "Stand still and hit it! Stand still!"

If you're riding, you can't move all over a horse and control your ride. Think like a boxer. Betty went to boxing matches in Palm Beach with Armour. He would point out that the knockout power is in the short punches, not in the long swings.

You really have to be still when you hit the ball. You're coming at a giant pace as you're going through the ball, and you need your feet anchored in the earth at impact.

Armour had his left eye shot out in a war. You talk about someone who took dead aim at golf, that was Tommy. He would look and waggle, look and waggle, taking dead aim, not hitting until he was ready.

Betty was honored to be in the first four—with Patty Berg, Louise Suggs, and babe Didrickson Zaharias—to be inducted into the LPGA Hall of Fame.

But she appeared as deeply moved years later when she was inducted into the Texas Sports Hall of Fame along with her old friend and teacher—me.

At the banquet, she was nervous. She was supposed to make an acceptance speech, but the right words wouldn't form. She leaned over to Dave Marr, who was the master of ceremonies, and whispered, "Help me, David. I don't know what to say."

He whispered back, "You know how to say 'thank you,' don't you?"

He made her laugh, and then she knew what to say. "Thank you."

A Story by
Paula Granoff

EVER SINCE I read Harvey's *Little Red Book* in 1992 and used two of its images—swing the club like a weed cutter and clip the tee—to win the Rhode Island State Seniors, the first tournament victory of my life, I stop off in Austin regularly to visit Harvey and Helen as my husband, Lenny, and I travel back and forth between our summer and winter homes in Providence and Palm Beach.

Last November I felt I needed to make a special trip from Palm Beach for a lesson from Harvey, because my chipping had become very poor. I phoned Helen, who relayed the word to Harvey. As he always does, he said he wouldn't give me a lesson unless I'd had my chipping problem at least three rounds in a row. I told Helen it had already lasted longer than that, and Harvey said for me to make the trip.

I arrived in Austin, went to dinner with Helen, Tinsley, and his wife, Betty Ann, and the next morning I met Harvey at the practice range. He watched me hit chip shots with my 7-iron for a while.

He said, "Paula, it's worse than I thought. I don't know if I can fix it or not. But I am going to try."

After a couple of hours Harvey's nurse, Karenza, told him it was time for lunch.

"No, I'm not leaving until we get Paula fixed," he said.

What I was doing was hitting behind the ball. I just couldn't stop it, and Harvey couldn't figure out what was causing it. My long game is better than it has ever been, but I had gotten to where I was almost afraid to hit a little chip shot because I didn't know where it was going.

Harvey said to me, "Paula, my eyes are not as sharp as they used to be, but even I can see you are hitting from half an inch to an inch behind the ball. Can't you see that?"

I said, "Yes, Harvey, I can see it. But I can't help it."

Harvey sent for a bucket of water and had me swing the bucket back and forth, back and forth, one of his favorite methods of teaching rhythm.

But still my chips weren't working.

I was willing to give up and quit, but Harvey wasn't.

"You're spending more time on little nobody me hitting chipping shots than I saw you spend with Tom Kite in a lesson on driving," I said.

Harvey said, "I feel as if whatever you are doing is my fault. I'll never have any peace until we cure it."

We had drawn a crowd by this time.

Finally Harvey said, "Paula, I want you to try something."

"Anything," I said.

"I want you to look up when you hit this next chip shot."

I wasn't certain I understood correctly. "You want me to look up? Are you sure?"

"Just do it," he said.

So I hit a perfect little chip shot I watched roll from the fringe across the green and stop a few inches from the hole.

Harvey grinned. "That's it. You have been so con-

161

cerned with keeping your head down that your head is actually moving backwards as you hit the chip, and so you are striking the ground behind the ball. Instead of staring at the spot where the ball was, I want you to let your eyes follow the ball so you can see the pretty shot. This is not a cure I would recommend to everyone, but it suits you as an individual."

I hit a number of excellent chip shots. Then Harvey watched me hit some longer shots and pronounced me fit to return to the golf course.

"Whatever you do, take good care of those golf clubs. They are perfect for you," he said.

He asked how my grandson, Ethan, is progressing. When Ethan was four years old, I cut down a club for him and told him to swing it like a weed cutter. I had Ethan clip off the tee without a ball on it four times before each regular shot he could hit with a ball.

Those are the only two golf instructions Ethan has ever had—swing the club like a weed cutter and clip off the tee.

Now, at age five, Ethan is hitting his 7-iron about ninety yards with a little draw. It's such a beautiful thing to see. I'm going to do my best to make sure Ethan's mind never becomes cluttered with all the technical, mechanical golf instruction that caused me so much confusion for the first thirty years I played the game.

After the chipping lesson, I flew back to Palm Beach with confidence and a light heart, eager to return to the golf course.

And those clubs Harvey told me to take good care of? The airline sent them to Guatemala City.

Uphill and Downhill

PLAYING THE BALL from uphill and downhill lies is difficult enough without trying to remember a lot of technical advice.

To make it easier, I offer two simple things to keep in mind.

First, make a practice swing or two to determine where your club is going to hit the ground, and take your stance accordingly.

Second, lean into the hill. On a downhill lie, you will be more onto your right leg. On an uphill lie, you will be more onto your left leg.

The average golfer never practices these shots, but practice is the only way to learn to play them without fear.

Scrambling

THE SCRAMBLE FORMAT, in which every player in your group hits from the location of the best shot, is a lot of fun and makes it possible to have tournaments using players of a wide range of abilities.

But a scramble can be detrimental to an average player unless you keep your poise. On the tee box, for example, if the top player on your team hits a drive a hundred yards past where you could hit it, resist the temptation to wind up and swing from the heels in a hopeless effort to hit a shot you do not have the ability to hit. Doing this very often can ruin the natural tempo of your own game.

You don't need to be a long driver or an expert iron player to be a valuable partner in a scramble.

Just sink a few putts or hit a few chips close to the hole and your mates will be glad to have you on their side.

The Golf Ball Test

MANUFACTURERS ARE TUMBLING over one another in the race to bring out new golf balls that go farther than the competition's.

Their colorful advertising is full of compression ratios and dimple counts and trajectory charts.

I still think the best way to show how far a golf ball will go is the old-fashioned drop test.

Take two balls out to a concrete porch and drop them. The ball that bounces higher is the one that you will hit farther.

Where There's
a Will . . .

SOME PEOPLE TELL me they can't find time in their busy lives to slip in a round of golf. I sympathize with that complaint in these days when it can take more than five hours to make it around a crowded course. In my youth we used to do eighteen holes in three hours or less as a regular thing, but of course we were walking, and this was before golfers learned from watching the pros on television that they need several minutes just to line up a putt.

But who says you need to play eighteen holes every time out? A brisk nine holes early in the morning or late in the evening is good for you and good for your game.

Or if you are in special circumstances, you can follow the routine of a fellow I have heard about from his professional at an elegant private club in the East.

This fellow goes to the club each day in a Rolls-Royce driven by his chauffeur. His clubs are already on a cart and a caddie is waiting when he arrives.

The gentleman goes out and plays one hole.

If there is a group already playing the hole he is scheduled to play that day, they step aside for him.

Then, at the end of eighteen days, the fellow turns in his scorecard.

You can always find time for golf if your heart is in it.

Compliment from
the Haig

DURING HIS BARNSTORMING days of matches and exhibitions all over the United States and Europe, proud members of the clubs Walter Hagen was visiting would always ask what he thought of their golf courses.

Hagen was a master salesman, at ease in any company, the person who made being a golf professional into a respected occupation.

His answer to the question regarding what he thought of the golf courses was, "In my opinion, this is without a doubt one of the finest courses of its type that I have ever played."

Checking Ball Position

BALL POSITION IS an easy thing to lose. One day it is right, and you are striking the ball solidly, and the next day you are slicing or pulling your shots without realizing that your ball position has changed.

Where the ball is played in your stance and how far you are standing from it at address are vital to a good golf game.

Shelly Mayfield, an old friend and pupil who was a good tour player and later became a top club pro at Brook Hollow, had an excellent idea of how to check his ball position.

Once, during a period when he was hitting the ball especially well, it occurred to Shelley to get a big piece of cardboard and draw on it the position of his feet and the position of the ball.

From then on, if anything started going wrong, Shelly could haul out the cardboard and place his feet on it and see if ball position was the problem.

This is such a good idea that I think everyone should do it.

Big Enough

I'VE HAD MANY women tell me they would like to take up the game of golf but they feel they are not big and strong enough to be able to hit the ball around the golf course with sufficient skill to produce a respectable score.

In reply I tell them the story of Lina Diebold.

Lina is five feet tall and weighs just over a hundred pounds. She started playing golf at the age of twenty-three in her homeland of Indonesia, using men's clubs that were way too heavy for her. One year later she got her first set of women's clubs, and within two years she was beating her husband, Joe.

Lina is now thirty-eight years old, and her handicap has fallen from 36 to 4 at the Hideaway Lake Club in Lindale, about eighty miles from Dallas.

She has been studying with Hideaway Lake pro Scott Blackshear and with pro Bruce Furman from Holly Tree in Tyler. This year Lina won the Holly Tree championship by ten shots and the Hideaway Lake title by fifteen, her seventh straight champion's trophy at Hideaway Lake.

Lina gets good distance from the tee by using a strong hip turn, and she can lay her ball close to the cup from 160 yards with her 5-wood.

So let me not hear that you lack the height or weight to swing a golf club. Anyone can fit into the golfing world.

A Prayer

Give me a few good lies, O Lord,
    and the poise to make my life shots work.

Give me a healthy mind, O Lord,
    to keep the good and pure in sight,
    which seeing sin is not struck dumb
    but finds a way to set it right.

Give me a mind that is not bored,
    that does not wimper, whine, or sigh.

Don't let me worry overmuch about
    that fussy thing called I.

Give me a sense of humor, Lord.

Permit me the grace to see a joke,
    to find some happiness in life
    and pass it on to other folk.

Monsignor Richard McCabe
at the Harvey Penick Award Dinner
honoring Congressman J. J. Pickle,
1994

The Natural Way

THE MOST NATURAL way to fit your hands onto a golf club is to begin by standing with your arms hanging at your sides. It would be very unusual for someone to stand with her palms facing out. Just stand there in a normal manner.

Now simply fit a club into your left hand, easily, without forcing anything. Extend your right hand out, as if about to shake hands with someone, and place it on the handle below your left hand.

There. You've got it.

For some reason most golfers who are inexperienced tend to come underneath the club as they approach the grip. Their palms are up. This puts them in a very weak position, which many try to hide by twisting their hands into the semblance of a good grip.

A good grip is very much like shaking hands with the club. You couldn't shake hands if your palms were up in the begging position, could you?

I want your left thumb to be slightly on the right side of the handle, mainly for support. I want you to be able to look down and see three knuckles on your left hand. I want the V's of both hands to point toward your right shoulder. I want your V's to be closed so that your thumbs are against the web of your hands, with no gap showing. This makes for solidity and strength.

If all of this sounds complicated, just pick up a yard-stick and put a golf grip on it, and you understand it at once.

Two of the best women's golf grips I ever saw belonged to the great Fort Worth amateur Aniela Goldthwaite, who was the first Texas woman to be a USGA chairman, and to the legendary Betty Jameson.

I wish their grips could have been cast in bronze for pupils to study forever.

Dressing

I HAVE ALWAYS believed in women dressing not only for looks but also to allow themselves the right amount of freedom to swing the golf club.

All sports have a right way to dress for appearance and for comfort. If a woman player feels out of place, she cannot make the best use of her ability.

Remembering Babe

I PLAYED WITH Babe Didrickson in her first exhibition after she signed a contract with Wilson and turned pro. Al Espinosa, a Ryder Cup player, was with us.

Babe was a female counterpart of Arnold Palmer. Babe was bold and confident. She hit the ball far. Galleries loved her.

In that first exhibition, Babe hit a 7-iron thin, and her ball skidded over the green. She turned to me and said in a loud voice, "Harvey, these greens aren't holding very well today, are they?"

Babe could tell the rest of the players in a tournament that she was going to beat their socks off and make them like it, because she was not only telling the truth, she was also drawing the most fans.

She was a great athlete in all sports and had a natural, powerful golf swing. In the lessons I had with her, I could, in all honesty, mostly just watch in admiration as she innately seemed to know how to hit every shot in the book.

The day after she won the silver medal in the high jump at the 1932 Olympics, Babe was invited to play golf with some famous sports writers—Paul Gallico, Grantland Rice, Westbrook Pegler, and Braven Dyer. They talked her into taking up the game seriously. She hit a thousand practice balls a day while making a living as a stenographer and pitching baseball for the bearded House of David teams in exhibitions. In 1934 she burst onto the golf scene as a genius and a crowd pleaser. She won her third U.S. Open in 1954 following surgery for the cancer that killed her two years later at the age of 45.

Babe married wrestler George Zaharias, and they had a happy wedded life. When I saw George shortly after her funeral, we both broke down and wept in each others' arms.

Know Your Own Game

No ONE SHOULD know better than you whether you can hit a certain shot or not. Do not let yourself be overly influenced by the choice of clubs used by your companions. If it looks like a 6-iron shot to you but the others in your foursome are hitting 8-irons, you go right ahead with your first choice. It's getting the ball on the green and close to the hole that counts, not ego.

Once you do decide on the distance and the club, believe in your own decision and put your best swing on the ball. Keep doubt out of the picture. Betsy Rawls was the best woman player I ever saw at this facet of the game. If she ever doubted herself, you would never know it.

Howdy Do

EXPLAINING THE TURN to my pupil Gene Kirksey one day, I did it in such a way that she still laughs about it, and, most important, she remembers it.

I said, "Gene, just stand facing me. Now turn to your right as if someone had just walked up beside you, stick out your right hand to shake hands with that person, and say, 'Howdy do.' "

She started laughing, but she did it.

"Howdy do," she said, sticking out her hand.

"Now," I said. "Someone has just walked up from your left. Turn all the way back around and stick out your right hand to shake hands with that person and say, 'Howdy do.' "

Gene did it. "Howdy do," she said, shaking hands with the imaginary person on her left.

Gene tells me thinking about Howdy Do right and then Howdy Do left has made the golf turn forever clear in her mind.

Howdy do . . . howdy do. You might want to try it.

Playing Pregnant

ANNIE NELSON, WHOSE husband, Willie, is the famous
singer and songwriter, has had two sons in the last few
years, and each time she kept playing golf almost right
up to the moment they rushed her to the hospital.

The more heavily pregnant Annie became, the
smoother her swing became and the bigger turn she
made.

I mentioned this to Cindy Figg-Currier, who was in
her sixth month of pregnancy at the time.

"It's the same way with me," Cindy said. "I feel that
my center of gravity is steadier, and I really have something to make my turn around."

The only danger I can imagine in playing pregnant is
if you overdo it and get too tired. Otherwise, carry your
little passenger around the course and enjoy yourself.
Who knows? You might be training a future world
champion.

Shut Your Eyes

CARRELL GRIGSBY WAS having trouble with her putter, so I invited her to drop by the house one afternoon, and we would see if we could straighten her out on the carpet.

It is easier to find out if a putter blade is square to the line on a carpet than it is on a grassy green, especially if the carpet has a design on it.

I asked Carrell to stroke her putter back and forth along a border on the carpet, making her back and forward strokes the same length. We didn't use a ball. I wanted to see where she moved the blade on her stroke.

Then I asked her to do it with her eyes closed.

"If you do the stroke with your eyes closed, you are going to do it however is natural. If your eyes are open, you are going to be watching the putter," I said.

Carrell stroked for a while with her eyes closed and eventually got the feel of it.

I often have pupils hit full shots with their eyes closed to teach them the feel of the swing without any distraction from the sight of the ball.

Pupils amaze themselves at how well they can hit a full shot with their eyes shut and at how quickly this teaches them true balance as well as giving them confidence.

The golf ball itself causes many of the problems with the swing and the shorter movement we call the stroke.

If you slow your club even one-fiftieth of an inch before it reaches the ball, you will not hit a shot to the best of your ability. But this is what many average golfers do.

They are thinking about hitting the ball rather than about making a full movement all the way through the ball.

The only time I tell a pupil to keep her eye on the ball during a full swing is when I want to give her something to think about that will do no harm.

There is a difference between looking and seeing. You can look at the ball and not see it. What I want is for you to see the ball without staring at it.

Practice strokes and swings with your eyes shut and you will understand the sensation.

A Mind Game

MARTHA WESTMORELAND, ONE of our club's top women players, approached me on the practice tee and asked if I would watch her hit a few balls.

After minutes of observing Martha hit nothing but good shots, I said, "You look fine. What is it you feel is wrong?"

"Nothing," she said.

I asked, "Why do you want me to watch you hit balls?"

Martha said, "I just want you to tell me that nothing is wrong."

Our women's club championship was coming up. All Martha really wanted from me was a boost for her confidence.

"There's just one tiny thing that I see," I said. "Let's make a very small adjustment in your grip."

I acted as if I were moving her hands the smallest fraction. In fact, I didn't really move them at all.

"That's got it," I said. "Now you're perfect."

Martha walked away with a big smile, and a few days later she won the club championship.

Patty's First Time

JIMMY DEMARET AND I played with Patty Berg and another woman, whose name is lost in my memory, in Patty's first professional exhibition match.

It was a bitter cold day with the wind howling, and only a few Eskimos showed up to see the golf.

Jimmy and I wanted to call it off. Little Patty said nothing, but her father insisted that we get out there and play as we had promised.

Oh, what a dreadful front nine! My hands turned blue. The wind whipped my scarf against my face. Jimmy was having no more fun than I was. Patty marched bravely onward accompanied by her caddie and her father.

As we reached the turn, even the Eskimos had gone away.

But Patty's father was very insistent that she not quit, so Jimmy and I trudged with her to the tenth tee box. The tenth was a downhill par four with the wind at our backs. Jimmy hit one solid and nearly drove the green. I was a few yards behind him, and Patty was quite a few more yards behind me, because she had hit her tee ball a glancing blow.

My teeth were chattering and my nose was running as I watched Patty addressing her iron shot, with her father urging her to do better.

Patty struck her iron. The ball bounced once on the front of the green and then rolled into the hole for an eagle.

I picked up the ball and said, "Nobody can do it any better than that. Patty, you're a great player and you're going to have a fine career."

Jimmy loudly and sincerely agreed, and we shook hands all around, and then Jimmy and I started walking back to the clubhouse on numb feet.

After a minute, Patty and her father came along behind us. I guess he was disappointed that his daughter's first professional exhibition was incomplete, but I knew Patty would show him wonderful golf for many years to come.

The Fifty-Yard Pitch Shot

WHEN YOU BRUSH your hair, do you grab the brush hard by the handle and yank it and snatch it all over your head? No, of course not. What you do is use deep, smooth, flowing strokes.

This is the key thought to the fifty-yard pitch shot,

which is an important shot for golfers of all levels of skill.

All you need to do is look at your scorecard and you will realize that the great majority of your strokes are either lost or gained within fifty yards of the hole.

At the old Austin Country Club on Riverside Drive, I used to take a glass of lemonade, a sand wedge, and a bag of practice balls and go down by the big tree and hit pitch shots for an hour or so anytime I chose to get away from the shop or lessons.

When Ben Crenshaw was a youngster, he would practice hitting his wedge different distances. He would hit the first ball ninety yards, let's say, and the next ball eighty yards, the next seventy, and so on until he was pitching it maybe ten yards. You could look from the nearest ball all the way back to the ball ninety yards away, and they were in a straight line.

This is how Ben developed the touch that makes him a great wedge player.

Betsy Rawls won one of her four U.S. Opens with a short, soft pitch shot over a pond onto a slick, sloping-away green on the seventy-second hole.

Even the best of the touring pros, like Cindy Figg-Currier, feel the need of a session from time to time in the fundamentals of the fifty-yard (and variations) pitch shot.

One windy morning she came out to the practice range. The first thing I had Cindy do was take her grip without a glove and then tell me how many knuckles she could count on her left hand.

"Two and a half," she said.

"You get no credit for half a knuckle. I want you to see three." Since the last time I had watched her, her grip had weakened a bit, which is a common thing.

Cindy told me she practices her pitch shots with her sand wedge to the rhythm of a metronome to get her sense of tempo. I like this idea, so long as you do it without bothering others.

That morning on the practice range I had her strengthen her grip by half a knuckle and grip the sand wedge at the end of the handle to guard against chili dipping, and then I asked her to square up her stance. I prefer a square stance for these shots.

"Should I open the blade a little?" she asked.

"No," I said. "Square it."

Opening the blade to increase the loft of the club is fine for experts but a danger for average players. Cindy, of course, is an expert. But in the wind that was blowing that morning, a square blade was called for.

If your stance is too open, you are ruining the way the club is made to be played. Cindy looked good to me when she squared up.

"More than with any other shot in golf, I want you to think about swinging a bucket of water when you make this short pitch," I said. "Make some practice swings to get the feel of fifty yards. Your backswing and your forward swing are to be the same length. Let's not see a short backswing and a long follow-through, or vice versa."

We made sure her ball position was correct, which is about in the middle of the stance. I asked her to raise her club a little more abruptly going back—but without spilling any water from the imaginary bucket—to make the pitch shot go high and land softly.

Soon Cindy was hitting pitch shots with her sand wedge not only fifty yards but also to other distances I would call out, each one an increase or decrease of ten yards.

Sometimes I would ask her to hit it the same distance twice in a row to be sure the first one wasn't an accident.

Going back to the fundamentals, Cindy hit the pitch shots like the top player she is. Though it was windy and damp and she was pregnant, we stayed on the range for an hour or more. That's the sort of dedication it takes to learn to hit this extremely important shot with confidence.

Where Do Those Strange Shots Come From?

IT HAPPENS TO everyone. You are playing along nicely enough, and then suddenly from out of nowhere a stranger appears—a duck hook or a chili dip or a bladed line drive or any number of other odd actions.

Where do these shots come from?

They come from your mind.

You don't lose your swing between shots, but you can easily have your attention distracted. Once trained, your muscles do what your mind tells them. If your mind is wandering or lacks a definite goal, your muscles aren't sure what is expected of them, and some very strange results can follow.

181

A Story by
Susan Watkins

Now I AM the University of Texas women's golf coach, but when I first met Harvey Penick in 1978, I could not have dreamed this is how things would turn out.

It was a critical time in my life. I was recovering from severe leg injuries that took me away from what I thought was my first love—tennis.

I'll never forget that particular sunny afternoon when I drove out to the Austin Country Club on Riverside Drive to meet with then University of Texas women's golf coach Pat Weiss and Mr. Penick.

Mr. Penick kept a book that showed which members on the course were walking and which ones were in carts. He looked at Coach Weiss and said, "If you two are here to play, you look healthy enough to walk."

Coach Weiss introduced me to Mr. Penick. He said, "I know your name. You're a tennis player." I told him I had played competitive tennis for thirteen years but my injuries had brought that to an end. I wanted to learn golf.

My whole new life started that day.

Mr. Penick and I spent the afternoon talking. I told him I needed a game to fill my athletic void. He said I looked like a natural at golf, because my coordination and balance were very good due to all those years of tennis. Plus, I am ambidextrous, which is a favorable quality for athletes.

As I became a better golfer and spent more time around Mr. Penick, I realized I wanted to teach. I told him I wanted to be just like him, only a female version. I started spending more time watching him teach and listening to his stories than practicing my own game.

I have been able to walk down some of the same paths as Mr. Penick as a teaching pro at Austin Country Club and at Cherry Hills in Denver, and now as women's golf coach at Texas, a position he held for the men for more than thirty years. I have tried to imitate him as a dedicated giver and communicator to all levels of golfers. It was a thrill for me to see his eyes light up last year when he heard I had become the women's coach.

I was sitting in the golf shop at the club one day years ago, listening to Mr. Penick talking golf, when all of a sudden his hearing aid went blank. He said, "I'm going to go get a new battery so I won't miss learning something new today." He drove off in his little yellow truck and was back in ten minutes with a smile on his face. I said he had driven way too fast to get that battery. He smiled and said, "I don't need it anymore. My truck hit a big bump, and my hearing aid came back on loud and clear!"

I took Mr. Penick out to the Hills of Lakeway so he could teach a golf school with Chuck Cook, Phil Rodgers, and Paul Runyan. At first Mr. Penick sat quietly while Rodgers and Runyan discussed chipping and pitching. Runyan was wearing a sharply pressed pair of slacks, a cream-colored golf shirt buttoned to the top and tucked in at the waist, and a pair of polished white wing-tip shoes. With his round wire-rimmed glasses, he looked very stylish. Phil, on the other hand, looked as if his clothes had been wadded up in the bottom of the closet. I have never heard Mr. Penick speak ill of anyone, but he did lean over to me and say, "Maybe they don't have an iron where Phil is staying."

Mr. Penick would be the first to tell you he cannot teach "feel," but you would think he was wrong because of the way he could talk you into feeling things. For instance, he would say, "Listen for the impact instead of looking for it." This was especially for all the women who had been told by their husbands to keep their heads down. Mr. Penick would smile at them and say, "How does your husband expect you to find your ball if you can't look up to see where it went?"

He would say, "*After* you clip the tee underneath the ball or brush the grass, please look up to see your shot, because it might go into the hole, and I wouldn't want you to miss such a beautiful sight. Remember—it's your eyes that see the ball when you hit it, not your head."

Mr. Penick always enjoys teaching women, because women really want to learn. They look at him with trust, rather than firing questions and digging for the "secret," as men do.

It's easy for Mr. Penick to spot the beginner, because she shows up for the lesson with two things in her hand—her driver and her purse. The purse because it goes everywhere with her, and the driver because she wants more distance!

Mr. Penick is not only a teacher of golf, he is a teacher of life. He says he learns something every day and tries to pass it on. Life, he says, is growth, not age.

Mr. Penick is a beautiful person who has touched a great many people with his wisdom and his goodness. I want to be just like him when I grow up.

Nicole Remembers

RUTHE HAWKINS ASKED if I would look at a girl she knew who lived in Gonzalez, and I made an appointment to meet Nicole Cooper and her father, Cookie, on the practice range at Austin Country Club.

I liked them at first sight. Nicole was a sweet, small-town girl, and Cookie was a proud and loving father.

"I usually don't allow the parent to watch me teach the child," I said. "But, Cookie, I want you to grab a pencil and a notebook and write down what I teach Nicole. I know it takes an hour and a half to drive here from Gonzalez, and I want Nicole to remember what I said when you get home."

I try to get smarter every year so I can become simpler in what I say.

"The number one thing to write down," I said, "is that when Nicole's left hand is placed correctly on the handle, she must leave it where it is. It's all right if she feels she needs to move her right hand a little for different shots or on different days when her timing is slightly different. But her left hand always stays in the same place."

Cookie wrote it down.

We spent the first hour and a half on her left hand.

When it was time for them to drive back to Gonzalez, Cookie pulled out his billfold, but I told him to put it away. "I'm going to enjoy teaching her so much that I should pay you for bringing her here," I said.

Nicole didn't try for the golf team at the University of Texas as a frosh, but in her sophomore year the coach at the time, Pat Weiss, let Nicole be a walk-on. Nicole won a place on the team.

Last summer Nicole and another University of Texas girl, Nadine Ash, were among five university students from all over the country who were invited to play on the United States team at the World University Golf Championship in Madrid, Spain.

Nicole's game was in a slump as the big tournament approached. We sat down and had a long talk to build her confidence. Nicole has plenty of courage and needs only to believe in herself.

As Nicole was leaving, she said, "I want you to know that in Spain I will be thinking about you and what you have told me."

"No! No! Don't be thinking about me," I said. "You think about taking dead aim!"

Nicole won the tournament as an individual, and the United States won as a team.

When she came home, she showed me her yardage book from La Herrer'a Club de Golf.

On the last two holes, where pressure figured to be the most severe if she was close to the lead, Nicole had written: "Take Dead Aim. Remember Harvey."

Tears came to my eyes when I saw that, and I felt warm and good inside, and goose bumps appeared on my arms.

This beats money anytime.

Our Daughter Sandra

SANDRA PALMER IS like another daughter to Helen and me. As is the case with a number of my friends and pupils, I met Sandra because of Betsy Rawls. Sandra was teaching school in Fort Worth when Betsy phoned and asked me if I would take a look.

Sandra drove to Austin every Friday afternoon and back to Fort Worth every Sunday night for a year afterward. She never missed a weekend. Summer vacation she spent with us.

I told her to walk and carry her bag whenever she played golf. She needed to build strength in her legs to create more power and hit the ball farther.

One day I was giving a lesson to Governor Alan Shivers at our club on Riverside Drive, and we saw little Sandra struggling with her big red leather golf bag on her back.

Governor Shivers said, "That girl needs to be riding in a cart."

I said, "No sir, she needs to be getting stronger."

The governor looked at me and said, "Harvey, would you want your own daughter out there carrying a huge bag like that?"

I said, "No sir, I guess not."

I sent a cart for Sandra. But when she came in after her round, I pulled her aside and said, "Go in the shop and pick out a little carry bag and use that around here from now on. I want you walking, not riding."

After a year with Helen and me, Sandra went on the pro tour. Nowadays most young women join the pro tour after a career of playing in tournaments on their college golf teams. They already know a lot about competition. But Sandra had to learn to play golf on the tour against the best in the game. It was a rough introduction.

Sandra would phone often from tournament sites around the country. I recall once she called and said, "Harvey, help me. I am skying my tee shots."

I asked her, "How many?"

She said, "I did it four times today."

I said, "I bet you missed more putts than you did drives."

That put her mind where it needed to be.

She phoned the night before she won the U.S. Open. She needed reassurance.

I told her, "Are you just wishing to win, or do you really have the desire?"

"I have the desire," she said.

I said, "Then let God's hand rest on your shoulder, and if it is your turn to win, you will win."

Those are the swing thoughts to carry with you for a lifetime.